ELIZABETH SMART

WOMEN WHO ROCK series

ELIZABETH SMART

A Fugue Essay on Women and Creativity

KIM ECHLIN

Women's Press
Toronto

Elizabeth Smart: A Fugue Essay on Women and Creativity
Kim Echlin

First published in 2004 by
Women's Press, an imprint of Canadian Scholars' Press Inc.
180 Bloor Street West, Suite 801
Toronto, Ontario
M5S 2V6

www.womenspress.ca

Canadian Scholars' Press/Women's Press gratefully acknowledges financial support for our publishing
activities from the Ontario Arts Council, the Canada Council for the Arts, and the Government of Canada
through the Book Publishing Industry Development Program (BPIDP).

The author gratefully acknowledges the support of The Canada Council.

National Library of Canada Cataloguing in Publication Data

Echlin, Kim A., 1955-
Elizabeth Smart : a fugue essay on women and creativity / Kim Echlin.

ISBN 0-88961-442-3 (pbk.)

1. Smart, Elizabeth, 1913-1986—Biography.
2. Authors, Canadian—20th century—Biography. I. Title.

PS8537.M37Z63 2004   C818'.5409   C2004-901881-7

Cover design, text design and layout: Susan Thomas/Digital Zone
Cover photo: Michael Wickham, "Elizabeth at Tilty Mill"

04 05 06 07 08   5 4 3 2 1

Printed and bound in Canada by AGMV Marquis Imprimeur Inc.

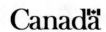

For Madeleine L. Echlin

TABLE OF CONTENTS

Prelude   1

Unconcealed   8
Youth   10
Put It All Down   14
What Can't You Write About?   25
The Marriage Solution   28
All the Drowning Women   32
Impotence   33
Voice   38
Turning Point   44
Independence   49
All Woman   52
Dig a Grave and Let Us Bury Our Mother   60
Lists: The Will Toward Individuality   63
Kenning: A Woman Artist Makes Her Own Patterns   67
A Dark House and a Whip   71
In Love   72
That Silence   77
Out of Wedlock   81
Birth   82

Fragment   89
New Terrain   90
A Mother Needs an Income   105
Published!   108
Self-absorbed   113
"I"   114
All Female   121
A New Plot   125
Lists   138
Inventing a Life   143
The Girl Voice   154
The Mother Voice   156
Soho   161
The Silent Years   166
Speaking Up   177
A Separate Self   180
"I don't think that *By Grand Central Station* is romantic"   184
Of Poetry and Gardens   189
I Am a Writer   197
Artists with Children: Another List   205
The Mother Book   207
What about Mexico?   217
The Last Diaries   219
The End   223
Coda: Past and Future   231

Acknowledgements   233
List of Photographs   235

PRELUDE

I had an interesting talk recently with a young artist. She said that the life of Elizabeth Smart does not interest her because women today don't need to be "so trapped" and "destroyed" by their relationships. As we talked more about lovers and children and art, she said she was worried about having children because she did not know how she could manage to have a baby and continue her work. Her concerns came tumbling out. She was worried about having enough time to nurture her child, about having enough time for her art, about money. She wished that she had accomplished more before "taking time off." She said that her lover did not share her concerns. He just figured he would continue working.

"Why have a baby, then?" I wondered.

"But I *need* to," she said.

The young woman was right to be concerned. After having a child, there never seems to be enough time. Work changes. Relationships change. One's way of being in the world changes.

Elizabeth Smart was a writer who had four children. She wrote of the womb's "duties, urges, necessities," and about how difficult it was to have children and be a writer at the same time. But she also insisted that having children was an impossible-to-put-aside part of being in love. Her passionate love affair and first pregnancy triggered an explosion of her creativity. She did not see herself as a victim of romantic love nor did she romanticize having a baby. She wanted to be in love with a man and she wanted to be a mother. In *By Grand Central Station I Sat Down and Wept,* she wrote: "He is the one I picked out from the world. I picked him out in cold deliberation. But the passion was not cold. It kindled me. It kindled the world. Love, love, give my heart ease, put your arms round me, give my heart ease. Feel the little bastard."

The idea of *picking* romance and babies was not something I heard when I was young. The idea that these things would *kindle* something new in me was unknown. All the young women I knew were postponing child-bearing. For many, their relationships were second to their work. Babies were considered to be a threat to a woman's success in the workaday world. Most of these things were left unspoken. There were few women in my life who both worked and had children. I do not think I knew of any artists who did so. Of my graduate class, I was the only woman to give birth to a child. Two others later adopted children, as I did too. The rest remained childless. A friend who attended a different university told me that she hid her pregnancy during the school year and gave birth to her first child in the summer. When a classmate asked her in September what she had done over the holidays, she said to him, "Nothing."

This same women, now an accomplished writer and educator, describes her years of mothering as sharpening her deepest connections with her sensual, emotional and intellectual life. Being a mother, along with working and nurturing other relationships, has been an integral part of her growth.

I like the Greek word for truth: *alathea*. It means "unconcealed." Why has a woman's experience of raising children and pursuing a creative life largely been concealed? Why is it hidden? What are the necessary conditions of creativity? Why is this truth so little discussed?

Elizabeth Smart loved the English language and she measured her own prose and poetry against the greatness of its finest writing. In a world frequently hostile to her experience of both body and mind, she wrote about male impotence, mother relationships, lesbian relationships, romantic love from a pregnant woman's point of view, and the difficulties of combining child rearing with art. All of these themes were unconventional in literature when she was young, and they were frequently demeaned by those in her intimate circles as well as by literary critics. During an interview in which she reflected on writing and raising a family, one critic cut her off with a dismissive "Miss Smart, you are not the first woman to have four children."

As a society we do not acknowledge how having children can lead us to new forms of creativity. But Elizabeth Smart brought this idea into sharp focus, insisted on the necessity of her own child-bearing and then struggled throughout her life with the implications of caring for her children. Much has changed since 1941, when Elizabeth Smart's first child was born, but, incredible as it may seem, essential attitudes about integrating children into our lives have not. When I had my own children, I began to understand and experience this.

In our culture, women and men expect to have adult relationships and to work, but we have no shared vision of how to nurture our children. Parents scramble with makeshift and changing care solutions for their children and adolescents. We have created neither parental leave that is adequate to the needs of a child in the first six years of life nor adult work-days that match the length of schooldays. We have not created high-quality universal daycare or indeed *any* universal daycare. Our universal early-education programmes limp along, cyclically threatened. Equally important is our adolescents' need for contact with adults who are not their parents. Yet, as a culture, we do not act on our obligation to mentor and nurture them. They thrive when we do.

We have acted on women's (and men's) need to work, but we have not insisted on the need for time to nurture our children. Neither do we collectively value doing it well or articulate a shared moral obligation to the next generation. Women still do much more of the domestic work than men do. We are still learning—at glacial speed—the importance of men taking emotional responsibility for their lives with children and partners and family.

The potency of children and creative life is a concealed truth.

༄

A young Elizabeth Smart wrote to her friend Graham Spry in England, "Be good. No. Be bad and repent." She left her home in Ottawa, lived with artists in France and Mexico, took male and female lovers, had four babies with a British poet. She never married. She created a self-exile in England during the Second World War, supported her children and various artists by copywriting, and recreated herself as a bohemian personality in London's Soho district. She wrote and published fiction and poetry. In the final two years of her life, she returned to Canada to write and teach. She was part of a tradition of women who act first and apologize later.

More than three decades passed between the publication of Elizabeth's first book and her next. Her own children were adolescents before they even knew that she had published a work of fiction. She spent years describing herself as a copywriter, a book reviewer, the mother of George Barker's children, but not as a writer. Why? Her first book, *By Grand Central Station I Sat Down and Wept*, was well received, and yet a common sentiment in her circles—only sixty years ago—was that women could not be artists. She completed *By Grand Central Station* in 1941, when she was twenty-eight years old, and did not find a publisher for it until 1945, a few weeks after the birth of her third child, when she was thirty-two years old. Two thousand copies were published, and then in the postwar recovery period it disappeared. It was not reprinted until 1966, when Elizabeth was fifty-three years old.

Her next books were *A Bonus* (1977) and *The Assumption of the Rogues and Rascals* (1978), two chapbooks, *Ten Poems* (1981) and *Eleven Poems* (1982), and a collection of prose and poetry called *In the Meantime* (1984). She saw the proofs for the first volume of her journals, *Necessary Secrets*, before she died of heart failure on March 4, 1986.

To write and to raise children one must, often fiercely, find the energy for both. Elizabeth Smart examined the potent tension between the desire to work and the desire to nurture. She vigorously defended the need to create conditions for both solitude and relationship. She worked with the paradoxical idea of sacrifice, the giving up in order to be transformed. She wrote in a late poem:

> Her Muse screamed
> But the children louder.
> Then which strength
> Made her prouder?

Elizabeth Smart insisted on the necessity of telling the truth—a truth that acknowledged female sensuality and having children, a truth that "unconcealed" difficult aspects of her female experience. At times her authentic experience was dismissed stingingly as self-absorbed or diminished as unimportant. She lived unconventionally and remained true to her resolve to write from her own experience in her own way.

There is no path to truth without sacrifice. Elizabeth Smart looked for it by living in extremity. "You never know what is enough unless you know what is more than enough," wrote Blake in his "Proverbs of Hell." Elizabeth Smart paid for living close to the gods. Anyone does.

UNCONCEALED

The road to Pender Harbour, British Columbia, was icy and black that new moon. It twisted along the edge of the ragged Pacific coastline; I could smell but not see the ocean. I was looking for the coastal village where Elizabeth Smart gave birth to her first child. When I arrived, the only bed and breakfast in the tiny village was closed for the season. Bone-tired, I turned off the car lights, sat smelling the salt brine in the profound darkness of the north and set about keeping from freezing until morning.

After a long time a pair of headlights appeared. The owners of the bed and breakfast had come home a day early from their vacation. They were surprised to see a woman alone in a car in the middle of the night. I told them that I was a writer doing some research in the area. They took me in and gave me an unheated room with a bed and lots of quilts.

I fell asleep.

I dreamed I was hurrying through a field and a priest stopped me and said, "You need a chapter on the Mission

Hospital in your book."

I answered, "I'm too tired. I haven't time for a new chapter."

Then a little girl appeared from the folds of his cassock, tugged my sleeve and said, "Don't be cheeky to the priest."

In the morning I awoke refreshed and jumped out of bed to look at the ocean through the bright winter sunlight. Winter ducks swam in the harbour. Old fir trees leaned away from the salt spray.

The owner of the house came to my room with coffee and toast. He sat on a chair by the door and said, "Well, if you're doing research on the area, this place has got a bit of history, you know. It's the old Mission Hospital."

I was startled. I asked, "What part of the hospital was this room?"

He thought a moment and said, "I'm pretty sure this used to be the maternity ward."

Darkness and chance had dropped me into the room where Elizabeth Smart gave birth to her first daughter a few weeks after completing her book *By Grand Central Station I Sat Down and Wept*. She was twenty-eight years old. These two essential acts of creativity, a baby and a book, marked the fulfillment of the longings of her youth.

YOUTH

Elizabeth Smart was born in 1913, the year D.H. Lawrence published *Sons and Lovers* and the year the Paris opera hissed at the opening of Stravinsky's new ballet about a woman marked for sacrifice, *Le sacre du printemps*. That same year, Canadian painter J.E.H. MacDonald painted *The Tangled Garden*, a picture of his own backyard. Plants grow off the canvas into the wilderness beyond the garden, as if no frame were large enough to contain its potency.

The Smart family encouraged all three of their daughters, Helen, Elizabeth and Jane, to be educated and to marry into means. A career was for the youngest sibling: Russel, Jr., the only son. By the time Elizabeth was an adolescent, she knew there are eight glasses of champagne to a bottle and she could quote William Blake. She was brought up to be a skilled hostess, a witty conversationalist, a wife and a mother. She memorized poetry and created little books of her own stories, including one titled *The Second Edition of the Complete Works of Betty Smart, author of "Wild Foods," "The Perambulating*

Notebook" etc. that opens with this witty introduction: "To begin with these works are not complete, and to continue with they are not works. But other people have made the same mistake, and therefore I am not an original sinner in doing likewise. In the beginning, hard-hearted reader, you should know that you will not like this book ...." She confided in her journals that she wanted to be a poet.

✦

I see the young Elizabeth best on the rocky Canadian Shield where the north begins. She is standing inside the wide, screened porch of her family's sprawling summer house, The Barge, twelve kilometres from Ottawa in an area known as Kingsmere. The house looks out over a lake on the eastern fringe of the Laurentian Mountains, in the Gatineau Hills in Quebec. Just far enough from formal social demands in Ottawa, the place is an oasis, next door to the prime minister's retreat.

Elizabeth is planning a bacchanalian revel and has written to the young art critic Donald Buchanan that her party will be "a true orgy" and that "reverberations of the scandal" might well reach him in England. She is planning it for a full moon night, Sunday, May 18, 1935.

She asks her neighbour, Prime Minister Mackenzie King, if she might use the mock ruins behind his summer house, a half circle of pseudo-Corinthian columns from a defunct Ottawa bank. She invites him to play the honoured role of Bacchus or Silenus. He readily assents to the use of his high field but sends regrets that he can't attend. Only a few months earlier, German troops had marched under Nazi banners through Saarbruck, and the prime minister is now fighting for his political life under the election slogan "King or chaos."

The night of the revel, Elizabeth plays Ravel's *Bolero* and Debussy's *L'après midi d'un faune* and some "wild Stravinsky" on a portable gramophone. Twelve guests, six satyrs and six nymphs, arrive at the altar decorated with wild trilliums, twelve golden cups and an enormous golden bowl filled with two gallons of claret and three bottles of champagne.

A tall, red-headed Bacchus, who sports a leopard skin borrowed from Government House, is played by Eric Mackenzie, an aide-de-camp. Charles Ritchie, just back from Oxford and preparing for a diplomatic career, sips from a flask under his coat. Graham Spry, who would soon found the Canadian Broadcasting Corporation, drives from Toronto for the party with his wife, Irene. He had responded to Elizabeth's invitation: "Is conversation to be in blank verse, free verse or is rime permitted? And do we bring our own glasses, or would we use an excoriated jack-in-the-pulpit or other idyllic and springtime vessel for the nectar?"

Elizabeth lights a bonfire and hands a lighted torch to each guest. They make a procession around the golden bowl, which soon lies empty in the dewy grass. Charles Ritchie later remembered that the thinly clad celebrants let out bacchanalian whoops while Elizabeth mimed a dance of the maenads. Elizabeth wrote in *Betty Smart's Book of Agony: 1936*, "In the encyclopaedia it said that in the Bacchanalian orgies of old they used to work themselves up into a frenzy and go at each other with their teeth. We didn't do that. The night was too cold and the nymphs lacked the proper fire of Bacchus."

The next day, after serving breakfast to everyone at the family summer house, Elizabeth wrote a polite thank-you note to the prime minister for the use of his ruins. She praised him for having made possible "the coming of Bacchus to Canada—a thing you will agree much to be desired."

❧

This was the last party she gave in Canada before creating her permanent exile. In her final diaries she recalled racing from her family's summer house to Ottawa, where she attended Government House parties, and then returning to her beloved woods at Kingsmere. Her childhood passion for the wilderness stuck to her like sap from a pine, Dionysus' sacred tree. She recalled "climbing trees & even when 'grown up'—sticky resin in hair …." There she experienced her own nature "unconcealed."

But, even at the end of her life, she was still unsure of the importance of writing down what she discovered of her nature. A few years before her death she wrote: "Is it of any interest to anyone? Think of all those old men bashing out their memories .... How about mine?" And then: "Mine do bring things back with great immediacy."

She had been much surer of herself as a young woman in 1943: "Poor women with their lost souls and their hopeless causes. Poor world with its security anxieties, literally dying for prestige, for beggar my neighbour, for pride, for vanity. I must put it all down because of all the other drowning women to whom no one has ever thought it worthwhile to speak, or to whom no one would speak."

PUT IT ALL DOWN

The psychological development of many girls is shaded with ambivalence about a girl's power in the culture and her autonomy in her relationships. The key to a girl's education (in Elizabeth's time and still today) is the women and men who mentor her. With each passing generation conditions for individual intellectual and psychological freedom shift.

Elizabeth was educated by the personalities and stories of

the women in her family, at Canadian girls' schools (modelled after British public schools), in her family's anglophile social circles, and by her love of nature in the Gatineau Hills.

The women on the maternal side of Elizabeth Smart's family had limited formal educations. They tended to live through men who had big dreams and they shared their husband's fortunes. They enjoyed high living and turned their own energies to social life and entertaining. There was alcoholism. There was a high regard for culture tempered by a higher regard for social status. There were recurring streaks of romance.

Of Elizabeth's relatives only Great-Aunt Harma never married. She fell in love with a young man who died in the Libby Prison during the American Civil War. She was engaged to be married seven times (some people say six because the first and last were engagements to the same man). According to the family lore, Harma never got over that first love.

Harma's sister, Great-Aunt Pyra, ran away to Pictou, Nova Scotia, with the son of William Notman, the photographer. She peppered her letters to young Betty with Edwardian cautionary rhymes:

Pins & needles
Needles & pins

Work away and
Atone for your sins.
If you haven't any sins
Just peg away
You May have some
Another day.

Their youngest sister was Elizabeth's Granny Parr. Her name was Katie Baldwin. She stayed home and married James Alex Parr, a swash-buckling lumberman who made and lost a fortune a half dozen times. He was a Green Mountain boy with Ethan Allan. Three of Granny Parr's children died young and one died in the Great War. She had nine children and she liked to say that she wasn't a good producer because one of her friends had twenty-four. The last baby that survived was Elizabeth's mother, Emma Louise, born in 1886. Emma Louise was her father's pet. He called her Louie and he made sure she got her grade eight education. The women in Elizabeth's family were interested in marriage and babies and social life. They didn't value education for itself, and tended to worry that it was an impediment to a woman's social aspirations.

Russel Smart, Sr., Elizabeth's father, lost his mother when he was six months old. He was left by his father to be raised by two aunts who ran boarding houses in Ottawa. He liked to entertain and instruct his daughters with stories of how he lived in a tent while he attended the University of Toronto and worked at Woolworth's five-and-dime store. Not only did he take his bar exams in Quebec and become a patent attorney, but he also took a certificate in mechanical engineering. He met Louie when she was working in a government patent office. He became a lawyer in patent law and founded a respected law firm in Ottawa. He is remembered as someone who enjoyed good conversation and the active social life that his wife created for the family. He was also a reader and was at one time the president of the Ottawa Drama League. His friend poet Duncan Campbell Scott wrote after his death, "I shall miss Smart, he was a member of our little dinner club and the source of much vital talk there for he was, as you know, decidedly to the Left; I never knew anyone who was so generous to his family ...." Russel Smart created for his family a feeling of "huge luckiness," as Elizabeth described it, and encouraged his children to take advantage of all opportunity. His daughters socialized with promising young men in government, and with the men who would later build the National Film Board and create the Canadian Broadcasting Corporation.

Louie Smart used the family's money to achieve bourgeois goals: large houses in the city and the country, servants, private schools, regular travel to England for Russel's legal work and her family's socializing. She gave birth to three daughters, and then suffered a miscarriage. When her fifth child, her son, Russel, was born, she turned all her energy to him. After her brother's birth, Elizabeth recalled feeling "... bewildered—wanting more love."

Elizabeth's early diaries record Louie Smart's iron will and her ability to paralyze the whole family before a social occasion. The week of Elizabeth's debutante party and her presentation to the Governor General was a particularly tense one in the Smart household. Elizabeth wrote in her journal that at one dinner party she suggested that their dinner guests move to another room. "Mummy said No! No! And went all sharp & livid & my insides churned up & down & I felt 'the hot digging-in fingers' ...."

I sense in descriptions of Louie Smart a woman who was much frustrated by her self-appointed job of steering her family through her own social ambitions. She did not value education for women. For her daughters, she valued social status above work and intellectual development. She wanted "more freedom" (as she put it) for her daughters but she was rigidly controlling. Her self-dramatizing letters, the stories of her frequent high spirits, the memories of her gracious hospitality, all point to an energetic, if intellectually unfulfilled, woman. Her child rearing included employing untrained girls to act as nannies, a common practice at the time. There was a certain romance around babies, but young children were quickly socialized to behave decorously in adult settings. Elizabeth invented imaginary twins named Simon and Raspberries to amuse her. There are also stories of Louie's children feeling bereft when she went on long trips to London, England, and New York. There are stories of Louie's impatience with mothering, of her trying to lock Elizabeth in a closet and smashing her hand in the door, of isolating Elizabeth in the nursery, of ripping her eldest daughter Helen's dress in one of her furies. Elizabeth made these notes about her childhood when she was sixty-five years old:

Born
Rejection
Despair
Incomprehension. Mouth hung open until 7 ...
Hysteria of mother. Anguish. Fear. Birth of brother.
Unpredictable storms that shake the whole life ...
Fear ... terror ... isolation

But no relationship is without its light side. Louie Smart's three daughters could draw her into moments of delight, usually at The Barge, where social rules were relaxed. In one prank there, the three daughters decided with their mother that they needed a butler to receive Lord John Pentland, a visiting British suitor. They dressed up the eldest sister, Helen, for the successful cross-dressing trick. But such cheery memories are thin. This same mother raged when things didn't go her way, withheld her love when she didn't approve of her daughters' activities, was capable of hitting them, and could silence them with the click of her approaching heels. After these outbursts, she would lie moaning on the bathroom floor in a pique. She seemed to thrive on high tension that ranged from outbursts of tears or lethargy to effusive petting and witty exchange. A former neighbour shook her head and recalled years later about the family, "There was too much shouting at the Smart house."

Elizabeth attended two schools: Elmwood, a private school for girls in Ottawa, and later, Hatfield Hall, a girls' boarding school in Cobourg. In all her years of formal education she did not meet a teacher who inspired her.

Elmwood was created for the daughters of Ottawa's elite in the leafy, protected, winding streets of Rockcliffe. Elizabeth was remembered by old friends in Ottawa as being "clever." She masked it. She clowned for her classmates, played at being a mother, adopted godchildren. She is pictured in a school yearbook pushing a baby carriage down Sparks Street. She had a reputation for scribbling other girls' love notes. One day in class she made the girls laugh when she dropped from her wooden bench and crawled up the aisle chanting "Barrie, Barrie, Barrie," the name of her favourite writer, the author of *Peter Pan*. After six years at Elmwood, Elizabeth's only diary entry about the place was that she was taught to say correctly: *"Honouh of the Mothah Countrih."* The only teacher she admired was Pegi Nicol, the art teacher, who was dismissed from her teaching position for riding to school on the back of a motorcycle.

After Elmwood, Elizabeth was a boarder at Hatfield Hall, a two-year-old Anglican school in Cobourg, Ontario. Again, there was no teacher who inspired her. Her music teacher, Noeline Storie, recalled, "I can see her at the piano in the dining room of Hatfield practising—strumming away with great vigour. I do not know whether it was a degree of genius or not but when I would remonstrate with her about the over-whelming disturbing noise, she would repeat over and over, 'I am talking to the Devil.' This incident is clear as crystal."

Years later in her journals, Elizabeth recalled that she was thought "clever" and she hid it, "made light of it, to try to capture popularity—a necessary camouflage, not to stand odd & conspiring, a figure, a painful figure of fun. Here the 2 faced business begins."

The Hatfield girls were required to go to chapel each morn-ing and evening. They lined up with their Bibles and wore white scarves that Elizabeth jokingly called "pillow slips" on their heads. Though she disliked going to chapel, the obliga-tory exposure to the rolling cadences of the *Anglican Book of Common Prayer* and the rhythms of the King James translation of the Bible marked her ear with two of the finest sources of English prose rhythm, and may have been the most important part of her formal education. She was a talented, highly indi-vidualistic girl trying to survive in a boarding school where she was being trained for society and conformity. She often felt a misfit: "I was secretive, cunning, bent on survival, devious. And later, decades later, developing those warmer qualities I reproach myself for not having had then, I regret this development for undermining my purpose (often mumbling *'par delicatesse, J'ai perdu ma vie'* ...)."

She completed her matriculation. The alumni notes report on her classmates' singing and music lessons, their debutante parties, their French and Swiss finishing schools. Only one girl in her class went to university.

By the time she was twenty, Elizabeth had travelled with either her mother or a chaperone to London for winter social seasons that were reported on in *Mayfair,* a Canadian social magazine. She had been a Canadian debutante, a ceremony she impatiently dismissed by saying, "You just curtsied to the Bessboroughs [the Governor General and his wife], and met interesting young men who knew about Proust." She had spent a semester at King's College in London and quit, disillusioned by "... long corridors full of listless girls studying to be teachers because they couldn't think of anything else to be." She had studied for a semester at the London Theatre Studio and given that up. She had given up her piano studies because her teacher, Katherine Goodson, didn't want uncommitted students or, in her words, "butterflies." But Elizabeth did not give up her detailed diaries and wide reading.

Her old friend Charles Ritchie wrote in his diary, *Diplomatic Passport,* "Few of my contemporaries, male or female, married young .... In those days we would have thought it a premature descent into the dreary world of middle-aged domesticity. As politics did not interest us, nor religion, nor money unless it fell into our laps, we must now wonder what did interest that generation. I can only speak for myself. I was after Experience. I lived in the private conviction that intense strongly poetic, dramatic Experience lay in wait for me. I longed for a condition in which reality lived up to Literature."

Elizabeth too wanted Experience. Both her sisters went to McGill University in Montreal, but she did not consider university for herself. She wanted to write. She was reading voluminously. She admired the moderns and read Virginia Woolf, T.S. Eliot, James Joyce, D.H. Lawrence and Henry Miller. She had not yet read Djuna Barnes and Anaïs Nin. This poem, scribbled in pencil on a scrap of paper in her journals, declared her ambivalence:

I am going to be a poet, I said
But even as I said it I felt
The round softness of my breasts
and my mind wandered and wavered
Back to the earthly things
and the swooning warmth of being loved.
Bright and hard and meticulously observant
My brain was to be
A mirror reflecting things out

in the eternal rightness
But before I could chisel the
First word of a concrete poem
My breasts fell voluptuously
into my hand
and I remembered I was a woman.

Elizabeth felt her body and her inner nature most deeply in the woods. She loved the untouched wilderness and objected to Prime Minister Mackenzie King cutting down forests on his estate, which adjoined the Smart family summer home. As a child she made illustrated thumb-sized books with detailed descriptions of mushrooms and birds and plants identified by their Latin and English names. When she was fifteen, her father gave her 200 acres of wilderness in the Gatineau Hills. She built a little cabin, painted the door yellow, and called the cabin The Pulley, after George Herbert's poem. She invited friends to share her woods, delighting them with midnight feasts of roots and berries and mushrooms she had gathered herself. With her English friend Didy Asquith (née Diana Battye), she rescued a chained and mistreated bear from a roadside stand, and together they released it into the woods near The Pulley. Years later, Elizabeth wrote from her self-exile in England that Canadian green is "bluer than English green, harder and more arresting." Despite her mother's objections to her "mooning about in the woods," she discovered her own sensuality in the smell of pine and in glacial rock and in cold northern lakes.

Her attachment to the Canadian north remained with her throughout her life, even after years of self-exile in England. A few weeks before her death she told her son Sebastian that she regretted selling her 200 acres when she needed money early in her relationship with George Barker. It was a place she had loved. She wrote in her last diaries about "... Kissing worms .... A 1000 miles of woods & lakes & pre-Cambrian rocks, right up to Hudson Bay."

By the age of twenty, Elizabeth was committed neither to a "career" (for girls) nor to university. She knew that she was now expected to marry and she didn't want to. She did not know what to do.

She wanted to write.

WHAT CAN'T YOU WRITE ABOUT?

Change winds its way through the generations.

In 1916, my great-grandmother was forbidden by her husband to vote in the first Saskatchewan election that enfranchised women. At dinner, he ordered their sons not to hitch up the horses. My great-grandmother walked to town and she cast her vote. Her daughter, my grandmother, first told that story with a potent mixture of pride and shame at a family dinner some sixty years after the event.

My mother was born in 1922. She grew up on the prairies in a time and place where girls were expected to marry. In her small town, there was an unmarried girl who got pregnant and decided to keep her baby and live with her father in an apartment on the main street above the print shop. The town shunned her. My mother learned a lifelong habit of profound compassion from her grandmother, who invited the girl and her baby to tea and instructed the grandchildren always to be kind to her.

When I was young, I expected to live with a man before marriage, though in my community this still was not openly approved of. I absorbed from both my parents the idea that education was so important that I would marry only *after* I finished university. I expected to have children "late" and to raise them with a husband. But as I began to travel I delayed marrying. An unmarried aunt whom I admired and who had gone to university for the first time in her fifties gently encouraged me to marry. This was the same aunt who frequently reminded me that I was lucky to be educated and that my paternal great-grandmother had been illiterate. No one openly discussed any limitations to marriage, but it was in the air. I knew the writing of Virginia Woolf. I began to read new (and critical) narratives about marriage by such writers as John Updike and I well remember the hot-pink cover of Germaine Greer's *The Female Eunuch,* which my older brother gave me when I was a teenager. My mother and father supported habits of hard work, family loyalty, generosity and the importance of the inner, imaginative life. The women in my family tended to manifest their imaginative lives in their empathy for others. A life created outside of marriage in a lesbian relationship or unmarried with a "career" was not openly discussed, but I knew aunts who lived in both these ways. There were many unacknowledged and conflicting currents.

My eldest daughter was born in 1990. She experiences her own conflicting currents, as her younger sister will too. She said to my mother and me recently, "I'm not going to wait to have my children. I'm going to have them young and I'm going to work too." She had seen a programme on television that profiled single mothers—a biological mother who used reproductive technologies to become pregnant and an adoptive mother. As she discussed the programme her grandmother said, "Why not? Maybe not getting married would be all right too."

Today children live with biological parents, with divorced parents, with adoptive parents, with lesbian and homosexual parents. Children are conceived using reproductive technologies to single mothers and couples. A short generation ago, many of these stories would have been kept secret, such families shamed or shunned, unmarried women referred to as "maiden aunts" or "spinsters," and children born outside of a conventional marriage labelled "illegitimate." Today, all sorts of families are openly acknowledged. Today, grandmothers and their granddaughters discuss them.

THE MARRIAGE SOLUTION

In 1936, Elizabeth took a trip around the world with a woman's organization called the Associated Countrywomen of the World. While she travelled, she made lists of possible husbands in her journals. She fretted, "How can I possibly marry and sign away my life?" Her dreams reflected her fears: "I dreamt all night of people getting married ... and I dreamt of people dying and lying in coffins— ... Emily Bronte—she was wax and Graham [Spry] wanted me to kiss her dead lips. I wanted to but not while he was there. It was very intense this marriage and death ...."

Elizabeth was working as a personal assistant to Mrs. Alfred Watt, the president of the organization. They visited Hawaii, Samoa, Fiji, Auckland, New Zealand and Australia.

They continued on to Ceylon, sailed through the Suez Canal to Port Said, Cairo and Haifa, then returned to Plymouth, England. Elizabeth disliked travel with the imperious Madge Watt. She wrote that she was expected to be a "free secretary and companion and dogsbody" and observed, "... I didn't get paid for this as it was called *valuable experience.*"

The Associated Countrywomen was founded by Adelaide Hunter Hoodliss, a young Canadian prairie woman whose baby died after drinking unclean milk. She wanted to educate other isolated farm women, and the grassroots organization rapidly became international. Martha Bielish, who later became a Canadian senator, was a member. She said, "I could look up from my work out there all alone on the prairie and know that there were other women all over the world like me. For many of us, it was our only contact with the outside world."

Elizabeth's diary descriptions of the endless packing and unpacking for Mrs. Watt, and the stiff teas with each town's society women, remind me of Cocteau's version of hell: to drive around for all eternity in a black limousine with a red flower in his lapel. Elizabeth was shielded from meeting the rural woman with their real challenges. She was expected to remain in town at each stop and be a "good hostess." She wrote, "Dull, dull, dull, sightseeing, dutifully, never any time to breathe, to live, to enjoy, to revolt, to be vulgar, to feel, to know, to understand. I hate facts."

The only time she felt any enthusiasm for the trip was in

Israel, when she was able to get away from Mrs. Watt to spend some time with young people living in kibbutzim. She was interested in their experiments with communal life, and was attracted to their vibrancy. She noted among their books in Hebrew copies of works by Aldous Huxley, Virginia Woolf and Oscar Wilde. She thought of staying on but wrote, "I began to dissect the reasons, and I came to a conclusion, which is this: that I seek a mate, not a way of life." As for the trip as a whole, she wrote, "I call this a detour because it was only an excuse to put off for a little while longer the settling of my future. It is my long-winded excuse for never having done anything. An alibi, in fact."

At twenty-three, Elizabeth perceived marriage to be a necessary condition. She wanted to be a writer, but she also needed independence from her family and the *only* way she thought she could find it was through marriage. This idea of marriage was so unquestioned in her circles that in all her voluminous early journals she never seriously considered pursuing her life without it. Yet she wrote that marriage felt like signing away her life. It must have seemed a terrible trap.

I try to imagine Elizabeth's idea of marriage. She perceived her father to be "a voice of reason," but he was frequently absent, and Elizabeth said it was best to talk to him during cocktail parties. Marriage and domestic life clearly did not fulfill her mother, Louie, who was frustrated, moody and often short-tempered.

Elizabeth also knew about artist Marian Scott's marriage to poet Frank Scott and about her former art teacher Pegi Nicol Macleod's marriage to Norman Macleod. These artist-wives ran the home, raised the children and organized their family's daily lives, squeezing their own art in around the edges. They encouraged one another to keep painting, and shared their joy in their children and their frustrations about domesticity in a series of fascinating, life-loving letters, which have been published in *Daffodils in Winter*.

But neither model of marriage offered Elizabeth what she was looking for—independence and the freedom to work. Traditional marriage limited woman. Elizabeth's favourite novelists at this time—Virginia Woolf, D.H. Lawrence, Henry Miller—did not idealize marriage. They explored unconventional attitudes to sexuality and they wrote about the limitations of conventional relationships. Elizabeth did not publicly reject marriage; she sometimes liked to say that she wanted to marry only one man—George Barker, the father of her children. Then she would add wryly, "I couldn't get him to marry me." But by the time her children were grown up, she usually said that she didn't want to marry him any more. Visits were enough.

ALL THE DROWNING WOMEN

In "Professions for Woman," Virginia Woolf describes a fisherwoman who says to her imagination, "... I cannot make use of what you tell me—about woman's bodies for instance—their passions—and so on, because the conventions are still very strong." She is describing the self-censorship a writer experiences when she fears that what she writes will not be tolerated by the readers of her time and culture, a fear with which Elizabeth also struggled. Similarly, Elizabeth would worry throughout her journals about whether *her* point of view could be of any interest to anyone.

A generation after Woolf's essay was published, Ursula Le Guin reflects on related ideas in an essay called "The Fisherwoman's Daughter." She creates a child to talk with Woolf's reeled-in imagination. The child says that she wants to write and she won't wait to do it until her children grow up. She says, "The one thing a writer has to have is a pencil and some paper. That's enough, so long as she knows that she and she alone is in charge of that pencil and responsible, she and she alone, for what it writes on paper."

Let us now imagine the fisherwoman's granddaughter. She was born being told she could do anything. Like her mother, she wants to have it all—children and writing and artistic freedom. Her world feels like a cracked-open egg. Yet this granddaughter sometimes feels constrained too. Why?

George Eliot observed at the end of *Middlemarch*, "... there is no creature whose inward being is so strong that it is not greatly determined by what lies outside it ...." The fisher-woman's granddaughter knows about her grandmother's and mother's self-censorship. She gazes deep into the water and hopes for a reader (and a publisher) with well-stocked minds. She wonders if she has the confidence to write the truth. She asks, "Are there still things that are felt but cannot be written?"

The two older women look at her and say, "Only if you do not write them."

IMPOTENCE

The novella *My Lover John* was the first manuscript Elizabeth sent to a professional editor. She did so under the pseudonym Lorna Parr (Parr was her mother's maiden name). The manuscript was inspired by Elizabeth's brief courtship with John Pentland, who had been considered a possible matrimonial choice for Elizabeth. He was the same British lord for whom the sisters provided a sister-butler on his visit to The Barge.

The story, written in the first person, describes a young woman who wishes to lose her virginity with a lover who turns out to be impotent. The fastidious British gentleman named John lectures her on *honour* and *discipline*, but the unnamed narrator is a passionate virgin from the new world. She talks of their souls "merging." She imagines herself into full-blown passionate states. She is thoroughly sexual and witty:

> ... I would rush into his room, flushed, eager, remember-
> ing things that never actually happened, but might have,
> between us, and he would comfort me with this marble
> enigma of himself. What did he fear? Certainly a *stone*
> phallus is polite even in a drawing room.
>
> "My lust is upon me," he would say with shame when
> natural waves too great burst through his fastidious
> etiquette exterior.
>
> "Good," I would say without shame, but half-leering ....

When they finally crawl into bed, after drinking Ovaltine in dressing gowns by the fire, John "bubbled over impotently" and fell asleep. The intrepid narrator wants to salvage the night. She awakens him passionately.

> I loved even his thinness, his protruding bones, the boils
> on his back and neck which I myself had caused. I loved
> all of him. I accepted all of him. His unlovableness I loved
> most of all. My excitement began to rise. Anything I will
> dare, anything I will dare, I thought.

John forces the "vibrating string" of her body into stillness. But the supremely confident narrator is not discouraged. She sends John a book on sex and grows even more obsessed with him. She writes dryly: "... though he was not my love, he was fast becoming my world."

Buried in *My Lover John* is one single, perfect paragraph that shines through the rest of the overwritten prose like a Chekovian moment—a simple, eloquent gesture:

> Later, when the fire was quite dead, I got up and picked
> my torn nightgown from the floor where it lay and put it
> on inside out.

The story might have ended here, but the young writer adds a final psychological revelation:

I kiss him and remember my times of warmth towards him ... he went home. I went into the bedroom where I slept with my mother.

Elizabeth gave *My Lover John* to her friend Graham Spry and to her parents, as well as to an American literary agent. There is no record of Spry's reaction, though he kept the story. Russel Smart told Elizabeth that he thought the story might be libellous and Louie Smart pronounced it "drivel." The literary agent rejected it as "too near the knuckle," and suggested that "male impotence is no subject for a novel." Although Elizabeth received no encouragement at all, she continued her journal writing. She tried to write portraits of people using Virginia Woolf's *To the Lighthouse* and *The Years* as models. She turned to the fertile territory of her mother's family and tried out a character sketch of "Aunt Ellen." She wrote, "Could I make her a great character, always influencing but never appearing?"

In the late 1930s, she also began a lively correspondence with Lawrence Durrell. He accepted several of her poems for his literary magazine *Booster*, although the magazine folded before they were published. Durrell wrote long, chatty letters and encouraged Elizabeth to contact Anaïs Nin in New York, whom he described as "the first woman, really the first. That is why she is such a lovely monster." He told Elizabeth that her technique "flopped" but encouraged her to keep writing.

Elizabeth had already discovered George Barker's poetry in a Charing Cross bookshop, and Durrell agreed to put her in touch with Barker so that she could buy some of his manuscripts to help support him. She readily assented to this role in order to begin a correspondence with him. She did not worry about compromising her own development as a writer if she became another writer's patron.

Unlike Elizabeth, George Barker was surrounded by people who wanted to help him and who affirmed his desire to be a poet. When he was still a schoolboy, his mother borrowed money to buy him a typewriter. When he was an adolescent, T.S. Eliot read and encouraged his poetry. Later, Eliot found patrons for him and a job teaching in Japan during the war. By the time Barker was twenty-two, he had published *Thirty Poems, Alanna Autumnal,* and *Poems.* The prestigious publisher Faber & Faber had taken him on. From the beginning, George Barker had the loving support of his mother and an admiring community of successful, male writers. He was the youngest poet to be included in Yeats' *Oxford Book of Modern Verse.* Faber & Faber stuck by him throughout his long career.

In contrast, Elizabeth's writing was viewed by her family, in her words, as "an intriguing form of *petit point.*" She was raised to be a debutante, a wife, mother and hostess; her writing was seen as a hobby. I have combed the journals and letters looking for early encouragement. Though Elizabeth had written volumes of journals, poetry and prose, she did not publish. On the contrary, the self-assertion she needed to publish was actively discouraged. Her ambitions were undermined by recurring double messages: be educated but don't show off your knowledge, be creative but be socially decorous, be free but marry. It would take a powerful personality to write the things her imagination was bringing up from the depths. It would take a powerful personality to publish them.

VOICE

Before Elizabeth's trip to France in 1938, she wrote to Didy Asquith that she considered herself too old to "be a virgin." She was looking for experience after her unsatisfactory round-the-world tour. She left London and made her way south through Paris to Cassis with a group of artists that included Julian and Ursula Trevalyn, Jean Varda, the man who would be her first lover, and a future lover, Michael Wickham. The trip was her first without a chaperone. This new assertion of her independence was accompanied by a marked development in her prose style.

I was interested in what life was like for women with money and independence in the 1930s. I telephoned Arianna Helpes, one of Varda's lovers, and asked her if I might come and talk with her. She said, "Come over at three. I'll receive you in bed."

I brought a dozen roses and rang at her heavy door. A voice called out, "Please!" and presently the door was opened by a beautiful, frail, snowy-haired woman wearing a diaphanous pale nightgown. Her head was wound with a blue chiffon turban and she wore dangling earrings and four strings of pearls. She beckoned me to follow as she laboured up a steep staircase. Her body was long and still sensuous through the silk laying on each vertebra, revealing her lovely buttocks. At the top of the staircase she turned into her bedroom, climbed up on the big bed and settled herself with a heavy sigh against a cloud of pillows. Books and dishes, a telephone, writing paper, letters and bills were stacked around her. She lived in bed. The decision to open the door downstairs was not one lightly taken. I thanked her for having me.

"Oh, don't thank me," she said, "I never do anything I don't want to."

I was to meet many women who spoke directly in Elizabeth's British circles.

She patted the comforter. "Here, get up on the bed. There, sit there. No, go put the flowers in water first."

Once the flowers were on the windowsill and I was again

perched on the bed, Arianna said, "I didn't know her, so I don't see why you've bothered to come."

I had come because I wanted to know about Jean Varda, Elizabeth's first lover, and about Cassis, the little French fishing village where they lived. Arianna described a small community of cultivated bohemians that occasionally included Vanessa Bell and some of her Bloomsbury friends. People drew and wrote and played music, fished and sailed and talked endlessly in cafés. Jean Varda was an eccentric, free-spirited Greek expatriate. He had left a secure profession as a portrait painter in Greece to build furniture from flotsam left by the tide, decorate his houses with collages of broken pottery, and fish enough to feed the small community in France. When Elizabeth first met him, he painted and he was working on mosaics created from tesserae, small pieces of cut ceramics and glass. His art was exuberant and bright.

"What were the days like in Cassis?" I asked Arianna Helpes.

Her intelligent eyes softened as she reminisced about long, lazy weeks with her Greek lover by the sea.

"Oh, walks, the little bar, friends, mostly artists, sailing every afternoon."

"But what did you do?"

"My dear, I don't think one ever caught anyone doing anything."

"But how common was it for a young woman in the thirties to go off with her lover?"

Arianna Helpes sniffed. "It depended on your circles. I was in art school. I did what I wanted. I was leaving a bad marriage. I had perfect freedom. No one ever stopped me from doing anything. No one cared."

＊

Anglo-Saxon society had not prepared Elizabeth for thirty-seven-year-old Jean Varda. He was travelling with another woman at the time, but he made no secret of his attraction to Elizabeth. Jealously, he called her a "vamp" for flirting at a London party, and afterwards, she wrote in her journal, "... I wasn't flirting, I was only talking, I wanted to know Roland. Even more I wanted to know Ruth. I could have 'flirted' with Ruth but at a party men are for women."

Elizabeth wrote that during the trip through France she fended off Varda's sexual advances, but when they reached Cassis, he "attacked" her in her room. She wrote that she "fought like a wild animal" and they "scuffled around on the dusty floor." But she ended this diary entry with a mental shrug: "The nightmares that night! The cold shuddering fears! Face fear. I faced fear. Ah well. Flowers much fruit." Then, after the first time she made love with Jean Varda, she described hearing the nightingale sing.

Today we might call this description of "losing one's virginity" a rape. But the interpretation of sexual relations and "romance" are as subject to fashion as other human practices. The culture of the 1930s frequently portrayed as "romantic" a woman being forcibly overcome by a man. Big band lyrics described women both wanting men and "fending them off" at the same time. Two popular films in 1938, *Jezebel* with Bette Davis and G. Howard's *Pygmalian,* portray relationships of sexual coercian as romantic. This attitude was not limited to popular culture. Anaïs Nin wrote in a 1938 journal: "... to be violated is perhaps a need in women, a secret erotic need ...."

Elizabeth recorded strong dreams after her first sexual experiences. She dreamed about being alone in a strange country, of a baby that "bewilderingly came out of the womb." She dreamed about walking in an Ottawa snowstorm with Varda, and being in the London Underground looking for a place to remove a tampon. She dreamed about making up guilty explanations to her family for being in Paris. In one dream her mother fell over a banister, and Elizabeth and her father tried to revive her by kissing her and they ended up kissing each other.

Elizabeth was exploring her sexuality. She was writing. She was not chaperoned. She was becoming what she wanted to be in Cassis: an artist in a bohemian community. She wrote to her parents, "This is an *ideal* life and I see no reason why I *shouldn't* finish *both* my books." To her old friend Graham Spry she wrote, "I am so happy ... days slip by ... & I can work at last unhampered."

The language of her journals exploded into the hyperbolic, metaphoric style she would develop for *By Grand Central Station*. She was learning how to write about the new connections she felt between her sexuality and nature and language. She was now *experiencing* what she had long admired in Andrew Marvell and John Donne's poetry, the power of language to transform and redeem profane love, to express both the spiritual and the sensual. On that Mediterranean shore she worked with "overflowing metaphors": "Beauty is holy. Beauty is earthly. It is God. It is sex. It is the momentary harmonious union of God with nature."

She was honing an original language out of this new experience of her sensual, sexual body. She wrote using images of earth and blood: "Sometimes the rocks bleed. Knowing too much, gathering such greatness from the pouring good I bleed. I bleed to attain my God, not impotent but manifest by a sign. Not crying under the unripe fig, or sorrowful among the scarlet poppies pressing to the sympathetic earth the head asked to accept and understand something too all-embracing for its trembling frame."

It was a turning point. Elizabeth had broken from her family, lost her virginity and found her voice.

Hitler made his "Peace or Destruction" speech on October 6, 1939. In the background is the thunder of a foot-stamping, roaring crowd. War spread across Europe. Elizabeth left France in the spring to spend a few months in her adored Kingsmere woods. She had intended to return to Cassis in the fall, but war made travel to France impossible. She was stuck living in her parents' home in Ottawa, with unfinished manuscripts and her lover across the ocean. Her mother urged her to marry and worried about the war. People everywhere were preoccupied with war. Literary journals began to shut down and artists were conscripted as soldiers. E.M. Forster later reflected that "1939 was not a good year to begin a literary career."

Painter Marian Scott recalled Elizabeth's visits to Montreal that year: "She came often. She wanted to go back to Europe but she couldn't. She liked to talk about poetry with Frank. All the men were charmed by her. I'd look out the kitchen window where I was getting a meal together for all the visitors and there would be Elizabeth, perched in the branches of a tree with flowers in her hair reciting Shakespeare to them. She was always quite dramatic. It was difficult not to be jealous. She was very beautiful with her blonde hair. I don't think she was capable of boiling an egg. She used to invite Frank and I to the Ritz for breakfast. He would go, but someone had to stay home with our child and that would be me. Frank was certainly attracted to her. Sometimes she'd come when I was there alone and we'd talk about children and books and my painting. On one of those occasions she brought me two books of George Barker's poetry. I hadn't heard of him at the time. She gave them to me and she said, 'This is the man I'm going to marry.'"

Elizabeth found a job writing for the woman's pages of the *Ottawa Journal*. On her first day at work she drew a tombstone in her diary. She was paid $2.50 a week on the grounds that she was a woman living at home and did not need an income. She wrote stories about missionary societies and female temperance meetings. In one piece entitled "A Remedy for Stuffed Shirts," she suggested that a maypole be erected for the upcoming visit of King George VI so that Prime Minister Mackenzie King might lead the royals in a spring dance.

She is remembered from that time as a young woman hummingly alive, someone "who could do anything." She turned cartwheels on Parliament Hill at the Press Gallery simply because she had "always wanted to do it." When Varda arrived from Europe with a red tulip, a blue hyacinth and a yellow rose, she dressed in white and entertained him in a room decorated with lace and silver candlesticks. She played hooky from work on the first day of spring to go out to Kingsmere to look for spring's first flower, the hepatica.

She appeared to be free but she was living at home.

She was a journalist but she wrote only for the women's pages.

She worked full time but did not making a living wage.

Her father wanted her to work but her mother did not approve of journalism for a "girl." Louie wanted her to "keep house." Louie and Russel made one of the last of their regular business trips to London that year, leaving Elizabeth to take care of the house. Louie wrote from England instructing Elizabeth to "train the little maids," and she lamented that they could not see how the "brass on this side is polished."

Elizabeth resumed her correspondence with Lawrence Durrell:

> Is it stodgy up there? Well, worse, probably. It is the most exhilarating, exciting, inexhaustible country in the world, physically, but there are no people in it, no poets but inarticulate ones ... all the people who might have been poets go into External Affairs and never speak again. Ottawa is full of happy married couples, snobbery and caution.
>
> Canada I adore but I'll die if I have to live here. It's like a huge mine full of gold but I haven't even got a chisel—

only hands. O it'll take hundreds of years. I suppose we'll
have to start to decay (being now raw and green) before
things will begin to happen ....

While her parents were still in London, Elizabeth climbed
on a bus headed for New York City. Her sisters Helen and
Jane were already there, living with a small group of Ottawa
expatriates that included artists Pegi Nicol Macleod and
Marian Scott. Elizabeth was enchanted by the dynamic
energy of the city and its jazzy language:

My America

All Whitman prophesied. History of film. History of
records. Jitterbug. Policeman pally. "I like your dress," the
girl seller said. The vast towers—the life, gaiety—here now
colossal life. England dead in a winding sheet. Canada not
even conceived.

The people—the strength and beauty, staggering
beauty—the life—the becoming, the IS, the now. The fun:
pick-up gangsters who motored me thirty miles. The
Negro girl in the Women's room. Policeman "makes a
nice change." Not hard pavements ....

By October, Louie Smart was back from England,
distressed that all three daughters were out of reach. She
accused Elizabeth of planning an unsatisfactory marriage to

Jean Varda. Elizabeth wrote: "She had phoned and was hysterical. If I were going to marry Yanko [Jean Varda] she might just as well commit suicide. I would have killed her etc .... I am glad I was out. But way below I am afraid she may catch me and drill her fierce bitter will into my escaping life, and I am troubled by her and for her."

~⊱~

Elizabeth decided to leave New York and go to Mexico to join surrealist painter Wolfgang Paalen and his wife, poet Alice Paalen, whom she had met in Paris the year before. They were preparing an international surrealist exhibition with André Breton. Paalen published and edited *Dyn,* an arts magazine in both French and English. The magazine published sketches by Henry Moore and paintings by Edward Renouf, and writing by César Moro, Anaïs Nin and Henry Miller. There were poems by Alice Paalen and experimental essays by Wolfgang Paalen. In one issue, Paalen published a survey on dialectic materialism that he had mailed to twenty-four intellectuals around the world, including Albert Einstein, André Breton, Robert Motherwell, Bertrand Russell and George Barker.

Elizabeth booked a steerage passage on *The Siboney,* a ship full of war refugees, and set sail for Mexico, away from Ottawa and her mother.

INDEPENDENCE

Elizabeth knew the family stories of her impoverished father who lived in a tent in order to go to university and she knew the stories of Great-Aunt Pyra who ran away to marry. When Elizabeth decided to leave New York against her mother's wishes, she was creating her own version of her family's independence stories; she was trying to live on limited means and to break from the powerful grip of her mother's will. She travelled with impoverished war refugees:

I said smiling when I had to lie on the canvas cot, and they vomited on all sides so that it splashed right onto my face, and the stench was everywhere, O I am in the thick of it. I love love love this my humanity, my people, themselves. It was so good—I was so escaped I smiled all over and said not one man am I expanded to, but all men and all women come what may, if they should do this or that forbidden thing I can but yield, I am all open and can offer no resistance—can only love.

Smiling, smiling, rocking on the rough sea on my rough bed—through the foreign language the friendliness the back notes better than through words—and most of all the adventure.

When Louis Smart found out how her daughter was travelling, she immediately wired the ship from Ottawa to request that the captain move Elizabeth to a first-class berth. Elizabeth was woken in the night while sleeping deeply, "as after love," and moved from below deck. She did not know how to resist the ship's captain or her mother's interference and she asked in her journal the morning after, "But could I refuse?" She worried about whether "cherished and guarded" she could continue her "great adventure in this familiar comfortable isolation."

In Los Cedros y Begonias in San Angel, Elizabeth discovered that Wolfgang Paalen was living with two women: his wife, Alice, who acted as his creative and intellectual inspiration, and his Swiss lover, Eva Schultz, who attended to his domestic needs. Elizabeth called the women his "two crutches" and immediately disliked Wolfgang Paalen's domineering and peevish temperament. She rejected his offer that she too become a lover and serve his art. She was unimpressed by the artists in his circles. She met Frieda Lawrence ("she seems to me now a photograph of herself") and César Moro ("his professional niceness bores me"), and she was not interested in anyone she met at Diego Rivera's birthday party. She was very interested in French "poetic prose" but not in surrealism. In Paris, the year before, she had bought a little book called *La Lutte Double* by Gisele Prassinos, a prodigy of the surrealists in the twenties. The twelve-page pamphlet is a collection of Prassinos' automatic writing that tells the story of a young woman consumed by an artistic movement. In a piece called *Rêve sous la mer*, Prassinos describes being attacked by surrealist imagery itself. She is in a station under the ocean filled with men, all reaching at her. Hundreds of eyes slowly devour her. But it is their fingers that terrify her most. They poke and prod. Finally the nightmare ends: "Tentacles pushed in spurts out of their great hairy fingers to penetrate: even after a big freezing wave tore them from around me."

The surrealists constructed love *(amour fou)* as an advanced form of automatism. They reinvented the idea of the *femme-enfant*, the woman-child who provides a direct channel to the sublime. Paalen felt justified in demanding that the women around him sacrifice themselves to his art. But Elizabeth could tolerate neither such notions of love nor the way the surrealists dismissed nature: "... they've used up the moon (they think) so they get their marvels out of (e.g.) a melting watch. (When I look at the moon not only my flesh, but my eyes, my hair, my bones, melt melt melt into the reverberating rays.)"

Elizabeth rejected controlling Wolfgang Paalen and his intellectual, but physically sterile, surrealism. She wanted to experience her own—female—body and language more deeply. She wanted to do this with Alice Paalen.

ALL WOMAN

An old woman talked with me in the deepening twilight of a September afternoon in London. She had known Elizabeth for thirty years but she did not wish me to use her name. After showing her torn photographs and telling her clear-eyed memories she finally said, as if testing me, "There now. What do you think was most important to Elizabeth?"

"I think it was love."

She shook her head impatiently. "My dear, you are mistaken. You must understand this. Elizabeth believed that only through suffering does one understand. She lived for passionate suffering."

❧

Elizabeth was looking for a voice that reflected her experience and she wrote about Anaïs Nin's *Winter of Artifice:* "... the voice ... ALL ALL ALL. And a WOMAN, a real woman, only by and from a woman, ALL. It fertilizes. It empowers."

She began to deepen her reflections on genre: "... I am irritated with the devious method and hidden indirectness of the novel, for instance, or even the short story, or a play. Poems, notes, diaries, letters, or prose such as 'The House of Incest,' in *The Black Book* [by Anaïs Nin], only meet my need." She used the imagery of sexuality and childbirth to describe the new form she was looking for: "But what form? Infinite pains for a poem. But I need a new form even for a poem. I have used up my ones. Tricks begin to slouch about. Each word must rip virgin ground. No past effort must ease the new birth. Rather than that, the haphazard note, the unborn child, the bottled embryo."

In Mexico, she experimented with adapting surrealist imagery to her own purpose: "The moon forced my mouth open and my teeth and entered me as I lay shaking on the brittle beige grass. Like a baby forcing the womb open its electric globe forced open my mouth. It was in me."

She translated Alice Paalen's poetry and prose from a collection called *Noir Animal*. She read with excitement Rimbaud and Gide and Baudelaire. French poetic prose paid more attention to language than to plot and character. In Alice Paalen's *"Le désespoir"* (dedicated to Pablo Picasso, who had been one of her lovers), Elizabeth learned how images can be held together by rhythm and the juxtaposition of images. She absorbed new ideas about style that she would adapt to her own prose. At the same time she read Lawrence Durrell and Henry Miller and George Barker. She loved modern English and wrote after reading Barker's poem "Daedalus": "It is the complete juicy *sound* that runs, bubbles over, that intoxicates till I can hardly follow (... 'the moist palm of my hand like handled fear like fear cramping my hand.' OO the a—a—a—!)."

Elizabeth's journal writing achieved a higher pitch of sophistication and excitement as the atmosphere in the Paalen *ménage* grew more intolerable. She felt flattened by Wolfgang Paalen's demanding and petulant self-absorption and she was troubled by his assertion that in order to create one must be unhappy. He ridiculed her wish to go back to Ottawa to attend her sister Jane's wedding and she finally rebelled at the household's condemnation of her bourgeois background and her pleasures:

> Why do they hate festivals so violently? They curse and deride them and want to sweep them all away. But festivals are the rhythm of daily life—the periods that make the dance .... Since the first man and the first woman need for rhythmic stops and gala days has been felt by human nature.
>
> ... Paalen reads books—begins to measure space—is the proud extoller of science—I listen—I *become* space— but I am "infantile" to be pushed out of the way when the real wonders pass by.

She received letters from Jean Varda, who chastised her for not caring about the war. Elizabeth resisted his criticism too. She was thinking about something she called her "mother-nature":

> ... I will obey my mother-nature's law. Her laws denied bring death. Love the flower by your side. Live, she commands ....
>
> If I feel swamping pity too, we shall both be submerged. But I am at all times her (nature's) instrument. I shall continue to look the other way. I shall dazzle his eyes with the sun. Fill his heart with love. Bind him to the earth with life, and if he still weeps, turn his tears to a personal pool, where he will not drown but lose himself in swimming.

She described Alice Paalen's moods as alternately hysterical or lifeless, yet she was attracted to her. When Elizabeth was finally fed up with Wolfgang's caprices, she decided to leave Mexico to go and live with Jean Varda in Hollywood, but first, she wanted to have some time alone with Alice. Wolfgang Paalen objected to Alice taking a holiday in Acapulco, so Elizabeth got a certificate from a doctor saying that Alice must go for her "nerves."

Sickness has been used by women from Florence Nightingale to Emily Dickinson to get what they could not take for themselves—privacy and freedom. Women in Elizabeth's own family frequently used a diagnosis of "nerves" to avoid unwanted familial or social demands. Elizabeth had spent a not altogether unsatisfactory year in bed as a child—escaping school to read as much as she liked—for an indeterminate illness that she referred to as a leaky heart.

Now, doctor's certificate in hand, Elizabeth and Alice flew to Acapulco where they freely swam and walked on the beach and talked and basked in the sun. On the fifth day, Alice asked Elizabeth, "Have you ever made love to a woman before?" Afterwards Elizabeth quoted Anaïs Nin in her journal: "That was the first time I ever tasted a woman ... I didn't like it much. It tasted like seashells."

Alice told Elizabeth about having abortions and then a baby at seventeen and how the surrealists were wrong to say that women scream with joy in childbirth. She described her baby's death at nine months of age. She asked Elizabeth if she was disgusted, and Elizabeth replied, "On the contrary, it makes me think how much of life I have missed not to have had a baby too at seventeen." She wrote:

> Her eyes—though—she was all woman—womanhood—
> her eyes then were worn, tired, sad, deceived, full of bitter
> knowledge, love, all the wonderful and terrible things that
> ever came to a woman—her eyes like this, naked—eyes
> my mother had after her long scenes of hysterics and

crying—but all the time her smiling dream mouth, smiling, smiling. "Have you ever been with another as you have been with me?" "No." "Never?" "Never." "And it seems natural to you to be like this with me?" "Yes." "Most women like men, some women like women, but it's rare to like both." "I like being," I said.

Once again, when Elizabeth experienced her sexuality, she dreamed about her mother:

I dreamt a long dream of Henry Miller and his friends and of escaping and indoor swimming pools and then my mother and a flock of sexual babies .... She said, Look! And she lifted her skirt and showed me how she had sewn her underskirt together into a kind of below-the-knees bloomers, with great untidy stitches in sailor's strong thread. She was defiant, but I touched her face and it was as hard as stone, petrified with fear. All over she was hard lumps. I was filled with compassion for her terror arisen from ignorance ....

Elizabeth discovered in Alice Paalen a quality she had never encountered in her Anglo-Saxon circles. She wrote, "Alice smells of white of egg and has a tender dry sympathy .... She soothes. She will be the world's lover-mother." Her prose began to include startling associations and images. She started her most daring experiment to date, a long piece about her mother and her affair with Alice Paalen called *Dig a Grave and Let Us Bury Our Mother*. The writing in this piece takes a great leap beyond her previous work. The first notes for her "mother-book" record episodes of violence between the mother and her daughters. The narrator-daughter describes her mother with images of war and murder: "She would have killed my happiness in my chaotic steerage life with one glance from her eyes like a firing squadron."

Though Alice Paalen and Elizabeth were alone together for only thirteen days, Alice Paalen loosed Elizabeth's clenched-up corners. The night before they parted, Alice taught Elizabeth a song of love and of learning to forget, a song about the *rossignol,* the nightingale. In the beautiful, suffering, poetic French woman, Elizabeth, a post-Edwardian, Upper Canadian, found what she craved—female passion:

> ... she entered the enormous caves. We are in the caves, warm, damp, fold upon fold, the caves bigger than the mind can hold, they hug the mind, enveloping, sinking it back, burying it in rocking softness. Or with my mouth I swallow myself and her.

The writing in *Dig a Grave* is Elizabeth's most daring, most original, and I think still her most thematically experimental. And yet she did not submit it to *Dyn* where it certainly would have been published. She did not submit it anywhere. To the end of her life, Elizabeth wanted to do more work on her "mother-book." To the end of her life, she called for her mother in her sleep and wrote about her mother in her journals: "So what is it about? Do I dare plunge into this journey?" This manuscript was a truth for which she could find neither form nor language. At the end of her life, she published her fragmentary thoughts about her "mother-book" in a piece called "In the Meantime: Diary of a Blockage." She wrote: "The Mother mystery has to come into the old age part .... Because it is the mother from one's childhood; and also *being* a mother, which, while it never finishes, becomes clearer as the years go on ...."

Strands of her "mother-book" weave through her reflections on aging and love and sex in *In the Meantime:* "It's easier to abandon your children than your mother—which is the memory of a hope of perfect human understanding, a oneness of course impossible, but a vivid unforgettable leaping hope, aroused again by passionate sexual love, but even *that* is easier to get over, being never so perfect as things were in the womb ...."

In the same collection, she also published *Dig a Grave and Let Us Bury Our Mother*, a work that revealed the connections she discovered in a lesbian relationship between her sexuality and her mother, and the powerful writing she could do when she explored the full range of her physical eros.

DIG A GRAVE AND LET US BURY OUR MOTHER

Dig a Grave and Let Us Bury Our Mother begins with the classic sea voyage. The narrator is escaping from an old, worn-out state to be reborn through either death or transformation:

> I am escaping. I am putting miles of sea, continents of desert and impassable mountains between us. But her [the mother's] fatal electricity cannot be avoided. It penetrates every insulation. Now there are revengeful dreams where she catches me and drills her fierce will into my escaping life. I cower stock-still, trembling with fright. If I hit back the pain is excruciating.

The narrator longs for the uroboric mother, the one who "smelt sweet," "sang lullabies," "was a pillow against nightmares." But there were rough intrusions—mummy's storms that were "direr than typhoons," and turned one's "insides to stone." These images belong to the destructive, dark side of the "mother nature"; they are the devouring witch, the wicked stepmother, the Baba Yaga in her forest hut. This mother-nature renders others lifeless as stone, erupts destructively like a firing squadron or a typhoon.

In a powerful insight, Elizabeth collapses the image of the controlling mother and a controlling male lover into one:

> Again, he is that electric hate, that contagious possessive-ness I fly. He begins day by day knotting my stomach at breakfast ....
>
> Is it this peevish boy who wields the weather over my soul? Or my mother's long shadow, her stinging underly-ing echoes echoing still?

The unloving mother infects everything. The narrator tries to bury and heal herself in another woman's eyes, which turn into a nightmare vision:

> Her eyes like this, naked, were my mother's eyes, terribly terrifyingly near—eyes my mother had after her long scenes of hysteria and crying, of pacing up and down the veranda, wailing in her uncanny voice, "I am going insane! I am going insane!" Or moaning as she lay soft and whale-like in a lump on the bathroom floor.

The narrator hopes that if she can experience a woman's love, she might finally escape the mother's "fierce will." But the lover and the narrator and the mother all fuse desperately into one struggle, bound on a frozen wave. There is no separation, no love and no redemption. They are joined in an eternal hell of swallowing each other, the umbilical cord winding round and round their necks.

Elizabeth finds an original cadence for her language in this work. Her technical control and her use of imagery is incomparably more powerful than in *My Lover John*. This is the end of *Dig A Grave and Let Us Bury Our Mother:*

> It is my mother I swallow. It is the repellent flesh of my mother I embrace. The ogre is in my bed. For living pity's sake I am kissing the one I fly from. It is a wailing child. I am older than the world, older and stronger.
>
> Pity rips, seeing the agonized need. Those flowery women with dewy faces in the morning. Those prostrate women in their great forsaken meadows, with their daisy chains, woven like Penelope's, rejected and scattered about ....
>
> Why are there so many stars and why are they so cold? Why is the night so empty and so like a great black pit? All about my room, like clothes, are hung my images, they are locked in bureau drawers; when I am alone I take them out to stroke. I wove such mirages. I dare not tell you why. They are my drapery. My naked offering was too visible.

Are you happy? Are you happy? Yes, we say, weeping with an unhealable woe. The palms weep too, and in the north pines. And the wind howls.

But my mother is in my womb.

This narrator, enduring her unhealable woe, is a figure more from Dante than from the English tradition. In her youth, Elizabeth absorbed the great rhythms of the *Anglican Book of Common Prayer* and the King James translation of the Bible. She was now reshaping the great rhythms of English prose to her own voice, body and experience. She was writing something new in 1940, and to the end of her life she never found a satisfactory description for what she did. She disliked the term *poetic prose* and called what she wrote "concentrated prose."

LISTS: THE WILL TOWARD INDIVIDUALITY

The narrator of *Dig a Grave* belongs to a tradition of female characters who defy the conventions of their culture and are not destroyed. They will not be constrained by the cultural roles assigned to them. Their quests do not follow the male hero pattern. In the stories of Gilgamesh and Odysseus and Beowulf, the male heroes stride forth from home, test their mettle in a world of giants and war and monsters, and return. In contrast, female questers leave homes that are too restrictive. They test their mettle against social conventions that constrain them. They carry their true homes within and when they transform themselves, they also transform the idea of home.

I will not admit such great characters as Antigone or Emma Bovary or Anna Karenina, or even Hester Prynne (all of whom fascinate me) on my list, because in the end they are all destroyed. In other words: No tragic heroines allowed.

A Preliminary List of Female Characters
with a Will Toward Individuality

Inanna: She is the literary archetype of all female questers dating from 3000 BC. The Sumerian goddess descends to the underworld to find her immortality and when she returns, she sacrifices her great love affair to save herself. She then discovers compassion, laments her loss and reinvents the idea of marriage; her husband spends six months on earth and six months in the underworld.

The Wife of Bath (*Canterbury Tales*, Geoffrey Chaucer): She has five marriages, and openly argues for wives' authority over their husbands. She is bawdy and honest and a great storyteller.

Rosalind (*As You Like It*, William Shakespeare): She disguises herself as a boy and forthrightly instructs Duke Orsino on the art of loving a woman.

Catherine Earnshaw (*Wuthering Heights*, Emily Brontë): She loves Heathcliff passionately, believing their love necessary "like the eternal rock beneath." But she won't restrict herself socially by marrying him.

Elizabeth Bennett (*Pride and Prejudice*, Jane Austen): She acts with "independence of mind" to search for individual happiness and refuses to marry until her suitor absorbs her views about relationship and marriage.

Dorothea Brooke (*Middlemarch*, George Eliot): She works at creating an intellectual life shaped to her own inclinations within the bonds of marriage and the restrictions of her culture.

The narrative voice in the poems of Emily Dickinson: She defies all conventional thought (religious and social) to honour her personal and idiosyncratic vision.

Lily Briscoe (*To the Lighthouse*, Virginia Woolf): She rejects the power of being Mrs. Ramsay, the female centre of the household—mother, wife, eternal domestic energy—in favour of becoming an artist and achieving a single stroke on her canvas.

Molly Bloom (*Ulysses*, James Joyce): She is not Penelope waiting chastely at home for her returning hero. She is virgin, wife, mother, lover of many and a performer—although in the book, she never leaves her bed.

The narrative voice of Anne Carson's *The Beauty of the Husband*: She is an intellectual with a passionate love of beauty raging against the betraying husband she loves. But she will not allow him to silence her.

Anna Livia Plurabelle (*Finnegans Wake*, James Joyce): She is archetypal feminine energy in the form of a stream making its way to the sea. She returns us to Inanna.

I place in this tradition Elizabeth Smart's narrative voice in all of her writing, especially that in her unfinished *Dig a Grave and Let Us Bury Our Mother*.

Elizabeth left Mexico in 1940 to live with Jean Varda in Hollywood. She mailed a pepper-tree leaf, to squash and smell, to her old friend Didy Asquith in England. She took dance lessons, and attended philosophy lectures given by Bertrand Russell. She could not write. She felt suffocated by Varda, as she had in the Paalen *ménage*. She wrote of "frustration" and "a numbness ... because it sees no image of success." She told Varda that his presence coloured all her "feelings, sights and reactions ...."

Varda openly objected to life with creative women. In *Collages*, Anaïs Nin records Varda and Henry Miller's discussion of female artists. They called Nin *une femme toute faite;* Varda said, "... I need unformed women, unfinished, undesigned women I can mould to my own pattern. I'm an artist. I'm only looking for fragments, remnants which I can coordinate in a new way. A woman artist makes her own patterns."

Elizabeth felt constrained by Varda's creative energy and

described the "loud ticking" of the male psyche beside her. She felt defeated by her writing and her blocked energy. She was a young woman who wanted independence from her family. She was writing things she couldn't bring herself to publish. Her diary entries describe her gloom:

> All my life I fight the glazed eye, the lethargy .... This evil, this sin, so monstrous in this descent—its jellyfish anatomy so known, so stale. It is just the flight of all delight, mystery and love .... A pall, a drugged relapse into the state of nonexistence—no pain except the fatal knowledge that life is embracing me and I cannot feel her touch.

Varda borrowed a shack in Anderson's Creek on Big Sur in California where a small colony of artists was living out the war. The sun blazed all summer, and in winter, wild rains and dense fogs sealed off the place. Buzzards hovered over thick forests of poison oak, skunks and snakes. In 1940, the coast was undeveloped. The artists rented former convicts' shacks with tin roofs and windows overlooking the sea. Varda scrambled down to the shore to gather mussels to cook. He turned an old iron stove into a fireplace on the side of a hill and made an outdoor bathtub from a wooden tub. He connected it to an oil drum up the hill where he could warm enough water for three baths and he planted fragrant roses all around. Whoever wasn't bathing sat by the open window and cranked the phonograph. Mail came from Monterey three times a week and fresh water was hauled from the waterfall. Elizabeth decided to join Varda on the coast, hoping to be able to write again. It was a remote, wild place, but it did not free Elizabeth from her melancholy. She could not even respond to nature: "I am frozen and it is not only Yanko's [Varda's] fault. I am guilty guilty guilty and the sin is the worst sin. Last night in the starry sky there was a terrifying long black rainbow, tubular and snakelike in the clear sky. I thought I could hear it roaring .... I can't open my heart to beauty, I can't open my heart at all ...."

What was she guilty of? She does not say. There was something profound shifting in the *zeitgeist* at this time that caused a number of female artists to begin to examine their "frozen" feelings, and to worry about what they were *not* saying. Virginia Woolf wrote in a 1941 letter to composer Ethyl Smyth that she could not write an autobiography because too much of her sexuality would have to be repressed. Anaïs Nin wrote of America (and its rejections of her work), "The climate of the forties was insular, provincial, anti-poetic and anti-European." Elizabeth received critical, censoring letters from her mother: "Betty darling, surely you are not going to be led by that effete and decadent crowd in California— cowards and traitors—where is your sense of proportion? Where your sense of honour, and where even your sense of humour? Who wants to read what they write when they dip their pens in the blood of younger and better men, to write."

George Barker's first letters from Japan began to arrive in the midst of this emotional bleakness. He encouraged Elizabeth to keep writing and said that he looked forward to reading her work. He offered consolation for the difficulties of the "emotional intestine" in which writers find their souls choking. His intuitive, writerly sympathies must have been welcome. His style was buoyant and alive. He loved language. He openly defied convention, especially the idea of "duty." He refused to serve in the war. In the postscript of Barker's last letter from Japan, he promised Elizabeth his heart and angels, and he promised to help her write. He just needed two fares to America. Despite Elizabeth's energetic solicitations from parents and friends and her own single day working as a maid to earn money to pay the Barkers' fare, it was Christopher Isherwood who eventually paid their passage across the Pacific to California.

A DARK HOUSE AND A WHIP

Romantic love is by definition irrational. It means sexual passion, the love of beauty, the potential for destruction, the taste of immortality. It is obsessive. Sometimes it flickers briefly, deliciously. Sometimes it lasts a lifetime, its destructiveness evident even to the lovers themselves. Yet, lovers are loath to give up romantic love. Lovers believe they are "most alive" in its embrace. With strange pleasure we watch "ill-matched" lovers devour each other; they believe that their love is their very life force.

I think about passionate, romantic love when I consider *Bluebeard's Castle* or some of John Donne's poetry or Wagner's *Tristan and Isolde,* or such novels as Tolstoy's *Anna Karenina* or Garcia Marquez's *Love in the Time of Cholera.* I think of a different kind of love—one that still has no name— when I think of some of Samuel Beckett's characters and of Rosalind in Shakespeare's *As You Like It.* Rosalind ironically and wittily says to the object of *her* desire: "Love is merely a madness, and, I tell you, deserves as well a dark house and a whip as madmen do; and the reason why they are not so punished and cured is that the lunacy is so ordinary that the whippers are in love too."

Elizabeth wrote this "ordinary lunacy" in *By Grand Central Station I Sat Down and Wept*. But her telling is extraordinary. Just as Rosalind tells Love in a fresh way, from a woman's point of view (disguised as a boy), the narrator of *By Grand Central Station* tells Love in a fresh way, from the point of view of an unmarried pregnant woman. But before Elizabeth wrote it, she had to live it.

IN LOVE

Elizabeth bought George Barker's manuscript "O Who Will Speak from a Womb or a Cloud?" for $25 in 1939. She had not met him but she had already told Marian Scott that she was going to marry him. She admired his poetry. She checked to see that he was near her age. She had always felt that she would marry and she said that she had deliberately chosen one of the best British poets of her generation.

No one has been permitted to quote from George Barker's letters to Elizabeth, though they are available to read in the National Archives of Canada. A few were published without permission in a book called *Autobiographies* (Tank Press, 1987). Barker's letter-writing prose style is poetic and erudite, often sexy and charming. His firm, spidery handwriting has a quirky elegance. George and Elizabeth's correspondence explodes with romantic passion and a shared love of language. The collection of letters tells a twentieth-century version of passion and betrayal.

Eleven days before George and Jessica Barker arrived in Monterey, Elizabeth dreamed that she was taking them from Kingsmere to Anderson Creek. She walked with Jessica, who was "small and sweet and rather silent" up a steep cliff and Jessica leapt over. Elizabeth went back to George who said, "Leave me alone." Then she ran back to Jessica who was still limply warm.

The Barkers arrived in Monterey in July 1940. By the last week of the month, Elizabeth and George were lovers. As in the Paalen *ménage*, George's women rapidly became two crutches: Elizabeth typed George's manuscripts and talked poetry, Jessica chopped wood and hauled water. But unlike the Paalen arrangement, this *ménage à trois* was not openly acknowledged.

At the end of September, Elizabeth and George left Jessica in Los Angeles to drive across the country to New York. They were prevented from crossing the Arizona border and arrested under the *Mann Act* (1910), also called the "white slave laws," which prohibited unmarried couples from crossing state borders together "for illegal sexual activity and related crimes." It was an act formerly used to limit the movement of gangsters, and was pulled out again for use during the war. Though the United States had not yet officially declared war, FBI agents were stationed at certain borders looking for spies. Barker's papers were in order and he was released. But Elizabeth's papers were not. She had not had her passport stamped on entry from Mexico to California and she was put in jail for three days. Her father intervened to get her out, while George Barker returned to Jessica.

After Elizabeth was released, she and Barker travelled to New York by train and stayed for two weeks. When Elizabeth returned home to Ottawa, where she had always arrived as the angel in the house, she wrote: "I look homeward now and melt, for though I am asked, what am I as I enter my parents' house but another prodigal daughter." Her life became twisted with lies. Her parents believed she had been travelling with both the Barkers; Jessica Barker believed that the main reason for the trip across America was to prepare a manuscript. Barker visited Ottawa furtively, was arrested and spent a night in jail for not having a registration card. He met Elizabeth in Hull, Quebec, and later in Montreal, then returned to New York. Elizabeth visited him in New York in late November. Jessica now admitted that her husband was having an affair with Elizabeth and she came East. There was a triangle of desperate, angry, self-justifying letters. Elizabeth's prose style became even more powerful:

> ... Asking no one's forgiveness for sins I refuse to recognize, why do I cry so for having my face again in Canada? The cedar trees and the chilly gullies with their red willow whips seduce me beyond control and envelop me too like an indisputable mother, saying Whether or No, Whether or No, my darling.

Elizabeth said that Barker's greatest gift to her was that he encouraged her to write exactly what she felt, something no one else had done. He assumed that "romantic" love was transient, and advised Elizabeth to note the detail and to record her feelings before the "initial intoxication" disappeared. Barker acknowledged the legitimacy of writing from one's sexuality. He wrote in the margins of her journals to "keep that vision" and urged her to defy convention. In short, he encouraged her artistic freedom.

No poet (especially one with as great a reputation as George Barker's at the time) had ever told Elizabeth she could write. In those first months of their romance he annotated her diaries, not without a certain arrogance, but always honestly. He praised her turns of phrase, wrote jokes and literary arguments and personal seductions in the margins.

The lovers liked to sit in bed with cups of whiskey and an ashtray and write together. There is an explosive vitality in those two inky voices talking to each other on the page. Sometimes Elizabeth took Barker's pen, finished his sentences and signed *her* writing with *his* initials—as if they were swallowing each other. In this initial "madness" of love, Elizabeth experienced herself merged in George Barker. But to say she was "in love" is inadequate. This famous, young, attractive British poet was encouraging Elizabeth's writing and her self-expression and her personal liberty, as well as making love to her. She had been "in love" with his poetry before she met him and now, in his physical presence, she was alive—physically, emotionally, intellectually, creatively. I understand this best when I think of Catherine Earnshaw's description of her love for Heathcliff in *Wuthering Heights*: "... he's more myself than I am. Whatever our souls are made of, his and mine are the same ...." George Barker was the part of Elizabeth who could write and who paid no attention whatsoever to the chatter of Ottawa (or British) society. He called her "elixirelizabeth" and "my heart my head my hand."

In December Elizabeth again visited New York for two weeks—and faced a painful thump back to earth. The poet Gene Derwood told her that she should not want to be a poet because Barker was one and that she could never be as great. Derwood said there are only poets, not male or female poets. Elizabeth disagreed in her journal and asserted that a woman is "overpowered by voices of blood each time she rises to speak her piece." She wrote about the "... beginning of that silence necessary for hearing my own voices, the voices of the thing I must capture ...."

THAT SILENCE

Elizabeth was now pregnant. I am fascinated by her identification of what she called the "beginning of that silence." She would live isolated through her pregnancy, and in a silence that would allow her to hear her "own voices." She would write and complete her first published book. Many years later, when her children were grown and she could again be alone, she would seek in the Canadian north once more that silence she had experienced as a wellspring of her creativity.

Elizabeth would not reveal her pregnancy in Ottawa where her unmarried status was unacceptable. She left by train for Vancouver on March 3, 1941. Barker travelled with her and they continued to write letters to each other even as they sat side by side on the train. Some of these passages would be transformed into sections of *By Grand Central Station I Sat Down and Wept*. This is a diary entry written as a letter to Barker:

... tonight we shall put the whole untidy world into a nest
and it will hang swinging comfortably as if it were far away
& as glossed over by history as the Red Indian's right to
be free ....

But O the glue of my mother's clutch. Can Freud
explain why it is stronger than the North East wind,
memory, reason or pre-Cambrian rock? No but it does
explain why certain angels have halos of singing birds &
Balder had mistletoe growing out of his heel. As long as
the accessories are such now as to make me a legend of
patience I won't lament that past I was when I could see
no future ....

Your concubine

E.

Elizabeth identified with her "mother nature" and refused
a world at war because she would "repopulate the world." She
would be nature's agent of renewal. But she wanted a mate,
and once off the train in Vancouver George could find no
sanctuary from his bad conscience over Jessica. He called out
in his sleep. Elizabeth wrote in her journal, "... the night
shakes him by the collar like a dog till he spits out the rag
ends of his fear, 'You're a cunt! You're nothing but a cunt!'"

They played at being sisters in front of the mirror,
wrapped scarves round their heads like turbans. "O, the glit-
tering incest bird," wrote Elizabeth as they spun out their

games and the images came crashing in on every side. Then they wiped away the lipstick and threw off the headdress and stood side by side before the mirror "two plain people ready for the night."

When Barker's friend John Fitch (with whom he was also having a sexual affair) showed up and left with Barker to drive back to New York, Elizabeth was devastated:

> It is not possible that he will not return. I sit here on one elbow hourly expecting his tight peremptory tap on the door. Each time the inefficient jangle of the elevator gets into motion, I start up. Will this monster stop at my floor and disgorge my miracle? I hurry back from a half-finished walk up the street. Are there any telegrams? .... I know that perhaps tonight his mouth like the centre of a rose closes over John's mouth burning with apologies of love like a baby at the breast.

Two days after writing this, Elizabeth boarded a steamer to Pender Harbour, where she was to have her baby. George Barker visited once. She stayed there alone for the last five months of her pregnancy. She wrote. She gave birth alone on August 28, 1941.

She had known Barker for thirteen months. All her life, Elizabeth asserted that it was because of George that she left Canada and won her freedom. She said: "George gave me the courage to break the surface bonds, to face the murderous act of stepping resolutely into my own life. Hearing, trembling with, her [Louie's] cries, her frantic unfair efforts to sabotage me, but going unflinchingly on."

These patterns—the judgement of Louie Smart, the inconstancy of Barker, coping with pregnancy, childbirth and taking care of babies alone—would continue for many years. Elizabeth had four children with George Barker. His wife, Jessica Barker, had one child that she gave up for adoption shortly after her marriage because the baby was conceived out of wedlock, and then she had twins in 1941. Barker had three long-term relationships after Elizabeth: with Didi Farelly, who moved to Italy (three sons), with Cass Humble, who moved to California and became a psychoanalyst (no children), and finally with Elspeth Barker, with whom he lived in Norfolk until he died (five children). I am not inclined to chart the details of how Barker managed this constellation of five "wives" (as the family referred to these women) and fifteen children. That is another story. Suffice to say that he lived a pattern of periodic appearances with all these women and children until he settled in his old age with Elspeth. He continued his writing and relations unhampered by any domestic responsibility. He did not contribute to the financial support of his children, was at times physically and verbally violent with the women, and frequently depended on them to support him. The women assumed all financial and emotional responsibility for his fifteen children, many of whom nevertheless kept up affectionate and warm relationships with him until his death. Elizabeth's eldest son, Christopher, wrote that when he was a child, Barker was "little more than a stranger" but someone he "still yearned for as a dad."

OUT OF WEDLOCK

It is important to remember just how unacceptable it was to have a child out of wedlock in Canada in the 1940s. It is equally important to remember just how unacceptable it still is, in certain circumstances and cultures. Birth control and abortion were illegal in Canada until 1969. Our social services are still required to support young women who are estranged from their familes because of babies conceived and born outside of marriage. Though we no longer have "homes for unwed mothers" run by religious groups, we continue to need similar services that have evolved from these roots.

In some places women may be legally stoned to death for getting pregnant outside of marriage, even if they are raped. In some places, women are shunned by their communities or illegally murdered by their own families if they become pregnant outside of marriage. Let us not be deluded that we are in a distant historical moment here.

In 1940, Elizabeth's Ottawa circles had solutions for "girls who got in trouble." They were sent away to have their babies and counselled to give them up for adoption to other families. These babies were called "illegitimate" and had no legal claim on their fathers. Abortion was illegal. Outside of the "homes for unwed mothers" and orphanages, society made no place for an unwed mother and her child, although women raising children alone was not uncommon. It was better to marry and divorce immediately than to have a child and to remain unmarried, even if everyone knew. Louie Smart wrote to Elizabeth during her second pregnancy advising her to marry and immediately divorce Barker, forgetting that he was still married to Jessica. Such was the power of marriage to legitimize a woman's life.

BIRTH

Pender Harbour, British Columbia, was far from Ottawa. There were no roads in. Everyone arrived by water—in fishing boats or lumber boats or by Union Steamship, six hours' sail and 100 kilometres north of Vancouver. The men who sailed the coast rarely travelled beyond the harbours where they were born. Some took boats up the reaches for logging. An old man from Pender Harbour showed me an ordinance map, tracing with his gnarled finger a wide inlet called Agamemnon Reach that dug deep into the north. He said, "That's the furthest I been. That's the place where God waits."

Elizabeth liked to say that she chose Pender Harbour blindfolded, by drawing a circle on a map and plunging in a pin. But Elizabeth was a survivor and practical. Somehow, her pin landed on the only settlement on the coast that had a hospital. She was able to go there, as she had travelled to France and Mexico, by living on what she and her family referred to as her "dress allowance." Her father continued to send her this allowance until he died. Increasingly, though, as Elizabeth wished to help George Barker and would soon have to support a child, her dress allowance would not be enough.

❧

I have an abiding love for expatriates who end up in isolated places. I have lived among them on the flat volcanic atolls of the Marshall Islands, on the tip of a peninsula in China, on a craggy fishing bay in Labrador where I was wrapped at night in a bear rug. They are travellers or entrepreneurs or biologists or labourers. They are doctors or dentists or nuns.

They are often loveable ne'er-do-wells. Whatever they do, I love their insouciant embrace of life.

When I visited Pender Harbour, I was enchanted by its rich history of expatriates. The Kleins, a quarrelsome German family, cleared the head of the harbour and called it Kleindale. After the First World War, Bertrand W. Sinclair, a writer of westerns, settled in Pender Harbour. The artist John Southwell, who painted the legislature in Victoria, lived there too. His son went off to China—no one remembers why—and returned home in a tiny boat carrying a woman and her expensive clothes, her exquisite collection of books, and a baby boy. The woman was Maximiliane von Upani Southwell. *By Grand Central Station I Sat Down and Wept* is dedicated to her.

Maxi was Dalmation, born in Austria at the turn of the century. Her father was a physician to the Emperor and had wanted her to marry royalty. The headstrong girl refused, married an Austrian engineer and followed him to China where he was working on the railroads. There she met John Southwell and she got pregnant. They decided to move back to Pender Harbour where they lived in a small fir-pole cabin on the salt flats. John developed Parkinson's disease and didn't work very much.

When Elizabeth arrived at Irvine's Landing, she rented a little house that was formerly used as both housing for the herring saltery and a small schoolhouse. Above the door she inscribed, "Does the cut worm forgive the plough?" She planted flowers in coffee cans and placed them on the eight steps up to the long porch across the front. She met Maxi in town and invited her back. Maxi picked up Elizabeth's dog-eared copy of Rilke and said, "I see we shall be friends."

Maxi had lived on three continents, in palaces and log cabins. She understood giving up everything for love and she understood being isolated with a baby. She became Elizabeth's best friend in Pender Harbour.

～

In the months of a first pregnancy a woman has utterly unfamiliar responses to the world. The sight of a child or a willowy girl or another mother can unleash tears of joy or sadness. The expecting mother feels alone. She is at the centre of the mystery. Her body bears at its core a fatigue so profound that she could bury herself in thick old leaves and sleep forever. People's hands are drawn to her body. They want to touch her roundness. Each time she awakens from those deep, deep sleeps she touches her rounding self and cannot quite believe. She dreams of death and feels death's intimacy with life. She embodies, for a moment, life's greatest mysteries: where do we come from and where do we go?

Elizabeth's most sustained piece of writing emerged during her first pregnancy. I do not think this is any coincidence. If a woman experiences any ambivalence about the "legitimacy" or "unfeminineness" of her intellectual or creative work, then the state of pregnancy and motherhood creates for her a clear and public image of her "femininity." The experience of pregnancy also unleashes in some women new feelings of power. Women have told me how they have undertaken and completed important pieces of work while they were expecting. They say, "I did it because I knew that after, I wouldn't have much time," or "I did it because I felt as if no one could tell me what to do any more." During my own pregnancy, I knew that I was touching a more physically powerful part of myself than I had known before and I wanted this power in my work too.

At the other extreme is the perception that a woman's pregnancy renders her "out of things." I felt this too, transiently. I sometimes felt as if I were in a liminal state. But just as we are not defined by any single element of our lives— a talent, the place we were born, an illness—so we are not defined by a pregnancy. Once, when my husband and I were trying to decide where to live, a colleague said to him, "Get her pregnant again and then she will live wherever you want to." Not many dare to say such things out loud any more, but these are attitudes that still float around. We live with all of these different responses to pregnancy.

Elizabeth did not keep a journal about her first pregnancy. She had to deal with Pender Harbour gossip, but not with the

judgements of her mother and her Ottawa social circles. I
think that the isolation she experienced at this time allowed
her to work fully and deeply from her deepest female self.
She was in the silence in which she could hear her "own
voices." She was alone and able to take time. She was also
working against the deadline of her baby's birth.

I know that today many women object to any whiff of
biological determinism in reflecting on why we behave in
certain ways. But we cannot deny our bodies or such essential experiences as pregnancy. I lay out these ideas, at the very
least, to openly discuss. A desired pregnancy can be transfor-
mative. An unwanted pregnancy is difficult. Why should we
be silent about these things any more than about any other
important experience? A pregnancy, wanted or not, changes
a young woman. After my first pregnancy, I said to a friend,
"I don't feel like my self any more." With deep-throated
wisdom she answered simply, "You're not supposed to."

On the night of August 26, 1941, Elizabeth's pains began. A
fisherman named Mr. Reid took her in his tiny boat to the
Mission Hospital. She looked out over the waves as the pains
rhythmically seized her. She always said that she gave birth
easily. The truth was that her first labour lasted for two days,
and then Georgina was born.

With children, life shifts into a different key. How to care for her children and earn a living, how to manage her literary work and her love affairs would be Elizabeth's central preoccupations for the next twenty years. Writing the truth about love affairs and babies, the oldest experiences in the world, was still new literary terrain. Even in the context of her chosen models—Anaïs Nin and Virginia Woolf—she was writing something new.

A tiny maroon Asprey's Graftonette diary, 2.5" X 3.5" with a slender gold pen tucked in the spine, is with Elizabeth's 1941 papers. In it she listed the momentous things that happened that year: she left Ottawa, she went to Pender Harbour, George Baker left her alone, she lived with Maxi, she gave birth to her first baby, she left her baby after three months to go to New York to look for her lover and "George didn't meet me in Grand Central Station and I had to go to Pegi Nicol's." Under "End Memoranda," she wrote: "This was a very sad year for ES—it was spent mostly in having Georgina—and the very great joy of it was turned into the most unimaginable sorrow." Nowhere in that list of the year's highlights did she note that two weeks before Georgina's birth she finished her novel *By Grand Central Station I Sat Down and Wept.*

Old letters and diaries leave the fingers grimy. The air from an archive's closed boxes traps the feeling of life irrevocably gone. I often felt melancholic as I sat under the archive's clean light, reading Elizabeth's diaries and tracing my hand over her manuscripts, handling objects that she had once tossed into her purse, touching the little Asprey's Graftonette diary.

What is left of a life in the end? Notebooks. A dead daughter's ring. Jotted thoughts shifting and transient as cells or skin. Musty paper. Words, always words. And a stranger sifting through the fragments and the shards.

FRAGMENT

Among her papers is the only response to the 1941 manuscript of *By Grand Central Station*, a long letter from George Barker. He wrote that the book was good but that he did not know what it was. He praised her highly for writing the "first true native prose poem in English." He detailed places where he found the prose too "loaded" with metaphor, or where it suffered from what he called "etymological fog" or "crazy syntax." He advised her that the craft of shaping lived experience, whether in poetry or poetic prose, was hard, "Flaubertian" work. He advised a more cohesive narrative. He acknowledged that she wrote out of pure sensuality. He affirmed her writing from her body, feet, legs and "genitals." He wrote that Emily Brontë, Heloise, George Eliot and Virginia Woolf would be the pallbearers at her funeral. This was the first detailed praise and criticism and clear affirmation of her writing that Elizabeth had ever received. Even years later in her journals she recalled her pleasure at receiving the letter.

But there was one thing missing. He did not offer to help her publish it.

NEW TERRAIN

Thousands of young Canadian women worked in Washington during the war years. The British preferred to hire Canadians, who were subject to the *British Secrets Act*. Elizabeth found a job in the British Army Office in Washington, first as an "office-girl," then, soon after, as a personal assistant to the Minister of Information, Harold Butler. Washington was conveniently distant from Ottawa, but closer to George Barker, who was living in New York. For the first time, Elizabeth was earning her own living.

I try to imagine what it was like for her to leave her three-month-old baby in British Columbia to travel across the continent. She would have had to wean Georgina, who was likely still not sleeping through the night. Her friend Maxi agreed to keep Georgina while Elizabeth got herself settled on the East Coast. When Elizabeth arrived in New York, George Barker was not at Grand Central Station to meet her, so she stayed with her former art teacher, Pegi Nicol Macleod. Pegi had a young daughter, and was struggling to raise her and to continue painting. Her husband was an alcoholic and difficult to live with. Did Elizabeth and Pegi play with Pegi's daughter? Did they talk about birth and nursing and all the things new mothers talk of? Did they talk about how to cope with absent men? Elizabeth stayed a short time, then headed to her job in Washington.

After three months, Maxi wrote that she could no longer care for Georgina because her own son needed medical attention. After a flurry of letters and telephone calls, Elizabeth arranged to have Georgina flown across the country in the care of a stewardess. Maxi got as far as the airport before problems with Georgina's immigration dossier were discovered and they were turned away. Then Maxi placed Georgina with a foster mother through the Children's Aid Society. How did Elizabeth cope with knowing that her six-month-old baby was being cared for by strangers? She quickly managed to get Georgina put on a plane to Washington.

Elizabeth still did not want her parents to know she had a baby. But the arrival of a "bundle of pink mystery" flying alone in the care of stewardesses made the pages of a Washington newspaper. Georgina Elizabeth Barker arrived in Washington on March 4, 1942. The next day a headline read: "London-Bound Passenger in Plane Provides Mystery at Airport Here." There is a photograph of a lovely, wide-eyed baby girl being passed from the stewardess to Mrs. E.G. Hastings, wife of a British Navy captain and an old family friend. The subtitle of the article is: "Motherless Infant Off to Join Father." When the reporter repeated rumours that the child was royalty, Mrs. Hastings told him a concocted story that the baby's mother was dead and her father was in the British war service. Elizabeth still could not claim Georgina because she had the measles. Georgina stayed with Elizabeth's sister, Helen, in Baltimore, until Elizabeth was well again.

Elizabeth disliked her office job and she was unhappy leaving her child with a babysitter. She complained that when she went home at noon, she'd find the woman sleeping on the couch. George was promising to divorce Jessica and writing to claim Elizabeth's "fecundity." He called her a "gold cow." He demanded that she kiss him in public on his visits to Washington and was angry when she refused to make him sandwiches to take on the train. She visited him in New York and became pregnant again. In the ongoing saga conveyed by letters among George and Elizabeth and Jessica, he wrote that his life was in Elizabeth's hands. Jessica was the mother of twins now, and George Barker wrote to her that his life was in her hands as well.

By the time Louie and Russel Smart found out about Georgina, Elizabeth had already found work in the British war office in London. It is likely that her father knew about Elizabeth's baby, as he had visited her sister Helen when Georgina was there. It is unclear whether he admitted what he saw, either to himself or to Louie. The family tolerated a great deal of deception. Louie Smart encouraged her daughter's emigration, saying that in England she would be "more readily accepted" and interpreting the move as patriotic "war work." Apparently it was better to go to a city that was being bombed than to be an unmarried mother in Ottawa. Elizabeth sent her mother a letter of farewell which did not acknowledge the baby but described her wardrobe as if she were leaving for the winter social season in London. She asked Louie to say goodbye to all the old family friends. She wrote, "... anyway, we were never a family to set great store by goodbyes and Occasions etc. so I know you don't mind."

She left and she never saw her father again.

Her ship was part of a convoy crossing the ocean. She was assigned to a cabin with six other women and two babies. During the terrifying trip, four ships were hit by torpedoes, and three were lost. Elizabeth's journal account of what must have been a nightmare sea voyage was terse: "... 3 weeks on ocean in convoy. Hits and emergencies. Scabies. Georgina. Pregnant."

Not until she rewrote this passage for *The Assumption of the Rogues and Rascals* would she flesh out her feelings, and then, only a little:

> I escaped by a hair's breadth the torpedo that seemed at the time to be a friendly if banal ender of my story. When the alarm sounded, I waited, with my daughter strapped into my lifebelt, full of relief, a kind of wicked joy, that I should be offered such an effortless way out of my pain.
>
> But that was not to be.

War. People remember the tip of a cigarette glowing in Oxford Street, a prostitute's flashlight like a glow-worm on Sackville Street, a sliver of light through a tear on a blackout screen. When Elizabeth arrived, she telephoned her old friend Graham Spry to come and get her at the station. He said, "She rang me at six in the morning and I took a taxi. There she was with enormous quantities of baggage, all alone, on the cold wind-blown platform, number six, with a child and vast quantities of baggage. That impressed me the most, how she got it aboard a ship in war I can't imagine."

Elizabeth went to visit her old friend Didy Asquith, who was living in the Cotswolds in a tiny village called Stow-on-the-Wold, a place little changed today. Rolling sheep pastures threaded with trout streams are golden in the late-afternoon light, and people live in mossy stone cottages. Even the soil feels used up there. Bones upon bones upon bones. Didy recalled Elizabeth's visit vividly when we talked together. They had their tea outside while sitting in the spring sunshine against the stone walls of the barn. She said, "Elizabeth had Georgina in a darling dress and the little girl spilled milk down the front of it. She just laughed and said, 'Oh, it doesn't matter.' We talked and talked about our babies, about the war, about George and my husband Michael. I had Annabelle then and was expecting another that summer too. Elizabeth was so lovely. She arrived and announced to me, 'These are George Barker's children and I'm meeting him in Kew Garden on July 1st.' I invited her to come in the summer and have her baby out here."

The next day Elizabeth returned to London and started work, leaving Georgina with a babysitter. A few days later, however, ministry officials discovered that she was pregnant. She said she was fired by a lady novelist for, in her words, "procreational activities."

Here was a dilemma in the 1940s: pregnant women were not allowed to work. An unmarried, pregnant woman without an alternative source of income was made dependent. In London, there were state-run clinics for free pre- and postnatal care, but a single pregnant woman could not earn money for rent or groceries.

Despite these difficulties, Elizabeth (who still counted on her "dress allowance" from her father) wrote buoyantly to Didy, "I continue to bless the Gods and all the Archangels that I am in England & that England is civilized. So far, I haven't encountered one draw back & everything is 100% better than I remembered."

She wrote letters and short journal entries noting that her old Canadian friends in London had "a welfare worker attitude to me." She wrote to Didy, "I can't think how to spend the next 30 years. What are you going to do?" She was not able to write. She abandoned a new piece of writing called *The Book of Lazarus* after a few pages. She was trying to establish herself in formidable conditions: a new country, war, rejection by her family, abandonment by her lover, caring for a small child, and pregnant at a time when pregnant women were not allowed to work.

Wartime in London meant standing at night on the rooftops watching the city's bookshops and cathedrals burn. Shadowy figures combed bombed cafes to steal jewellery from soigné corpses. Henry Moore sketched huddled, blank-faced people sitting in the darkness of the Underground. People later recalled the droning of the air-raid sirens as strangely bearable. It was the waiting, waiting, waiting for the next explosion that drove some mad.

Elizabeth wrote very little of her impressions of London during the war. There is only a poem she wrote to poet David Gascoyne on his sixty-fifth birthday in which, years later, she recalled sitting watching the bombs with him:

I remember I was there
When fire-bombs slashed the street
I sat on the stair
Beneath your feet
Two babies in my arms
And you read Baudelaire

As the flames leapt
And people ran with water
I clutched my daughter
And son, and wept.
You said, *"Le désespoir a des ailes*
L'amour a pour ailes nacré

Le désespoir
Les sociétés peuvent changer"
You quoted Jouve.
We did not move
Until it was all quiet
And we found we were not dead.

After Christopher was born, Elizabeth tried various solutions to combine work with taking care of her children. She shared a cold-water house in London at Hammersmith Terrace with a couple, and took a part-time job doing research while a neighbour helped with the children. However, Elizabeth was afraid of the air raids, so when the lease was up on that house, she took the children to George Barker's sister's home in Devon. When his sister went on holiday, Elizabeth found herself alone in a cottage with Barker's three nephews and nieces as well as her own children. There was no hot water and no sink in the kitchen. She wrote to her mother, "I think that housewives have the most miserable time of all with never a moment off." Her old friend Charles Ritchie offered to help her get a job at the BBC, and she put her children in a government nursery in Knightsbridge for three weeks to try to establish a home for all of them in London. When she got back, she was appalled by the children's condition. Georgina wouldn't speak and Christopher had lost weight. After that, Elizabeth decided to try to stay home with them. In 1944, she moved back to the Cotswolds near Didy

Asquith. In Condicote, she rented part of a house without plumbing called College Farm, on the village green. The owner of the house, Mrs. Foster, came in to help with cooking and washing, and her fourteen-year-old daughter, nicknamed Big Girl, helped with the children in the mornings. Even with this help, Elizabeth wrote little, but she did create little handwritten copies of George Barker's books. He visited periodically. All through this time Elizabeth was determined to get George to divorce Jessica and live with her.

One May morning Elizabeth received a telegram inform-ing her of her father's sudden death of complications from ulcers. She had been preparing to go with Didy and the chil-dren on a picnic, and she went ahead with the outing. She wrote in her diary:

> And of course the more things flowered the more sad it seemed & the nearer & more horrible death. I know that I am guilty because Daddy had me so much on his mind & I did always so much want to make him proud of me & happy. And he was so optimistic. And now things really have fallen apart & how can the centre hold .... I can feel the taste of death in my own mouth. But—there is never & nowhere a time for such a word.
>
> A form came for George from the American consul to emigrate to America to "join his wife & children."
>
> The evening by myself was horrible.

Didy sat with me as we enjoyed the warmth of the sun on the Cotswolds stones, remembering her life with Elizabeth a half century before: "She could bring out the best in anybody. I used to be impatient with my aunt who had thirty-six King Charles spaniels. She'd feed them chicken when we had nothing but bones to boil for soup. But Elizabeth said, 'You must understand, they're like her children.' She was very compassionate but she also had strong opinions and she would speak out."

I asked Didy, "How did you manage with babies, and the war, and blackouts, and no money?"

"We didn't mind. We both read Dr. Dick Reid's new ideas on childbirth and breathing techniques. We wanted to do things naturally. We ate raw cabbage and nettles for vitamins. But sometimes things were just too much. Elizabeth didn't know how to do things, neither of us did. We hadn't been taught how. We always had nannies and maids. Elizabeth was too ashamed to ask for help and she'd let the nappy pail get full of dirty nappies and maggoty and hide it under the bed. But it didn't matter, because we were living exactly as we wanted to."

Didy spoke of a hopeful, buoyant Elizabeth who cashed her cheques from Canada, and came back from excursions to nearby Cheltenham with presents for everyone. Didy said, "She had a lovely way of giving. She gave with such pleasure. I can hear that light voice of hers, her laughter." She remembered Elizabeth with her arms full of big bouquets of poppies,

lots of candles, and when the bombs fell opposite the manor on nearby Scarlet Hill, their songs to drown out the fear:

> When I wear my apron high
> He always passes by,
> When I wear my apron low ....

Didy said, "We lived very close to the gods. We felt invincible even though we had nothing. When you think back on it now, we were in a terrible state. My second baby was premature and there was no one to help. I kept him on the heater and rubbed him with olive oil. But we felt we were right and could do anything. When George came up from London for short visits it was lovely. We'd sit and talk and smoke and sing and read poetry. Then when he left, Elizabeth was desolate and we'd talk for hours about him and my husband. Elizabeth used to say, 'Didy, we just have to make our own little men-children because our own treat us so badly.'"

Didy paused, fell silent and gazed into the Cotswolds twilight.

When I met Didy she was caring for a granddaughter. As we talked, the child ran in after school. Didy rose, fixed the child's tea and, having run out of eggs, served a supper of bacon and fresh bread. We sat at the kitchen table and watched the child eat, talking of Didy's work, of old houses in the region, of friends. No life is untouched by sacrifice. Both Didy and Elizabeth had borne the unbearable loss of daughters. Didy watched reflectively as her grandchild finished her tea and ran away from the table. Then she turned to me and said, "We paid. Elizabeth and I paid for living close to the gods."

When Elizabeth moved back to London to try again to live with George Barker, she wrote to Didy debating the possibility of being both a mother and a writer. Didy replied that perhaps the best way would be to have two separate lives— the creative and the maternal. Elizabeth wrote back:

> I think you're absolutely right about the necessity of 2 lives
> for people (crossed out) women like us—& actually the
> lover-or-not with nothing to do but think about how much
> I resent George & need him & I realized how well (up to
> a certain point) I had managed ....

... I'd never have any tinge of jealousy toward any woman who once caught managed to escape. It would be Hope & Encouragement to have seen ONE example.

She wrote in her journal:

I am corsetted by fear. I can't move. I am mad with fear. Fear has driven me mad. I am afraid of the wind, the empty house, the air raids, burglars, lunatics, ghouls, catastrophes, sudden appearances, disappearances, death. I am most afraid of death ....

George—you must do something. I CAN'T stay alone in this house for so many hours. I AM GOING MAD.

It was a time when many women believed that men should be protected from the disruption of babies. In 1943, Ursula Trevelyan, with whom Elizabeth travelled to Cassis before the war, was also in London with her first child. They met and walked to the public clinic once a week to get nutritional supplements for the babies. Ursula said, "Elizabeth was very alone and very hard up. Her room was sordid and very smelly ...." Ursula and Elizabeth preferred to walk, even with Elizabeth's three-wheeled pram, rather than visit at home "because Julian [Trevelyan] didn't like to see much of even clean babies."

Elizabeth wrote to Didy that she felt it was her duty to create a calm home in which George Barker could create. She wrote of her second baby, "Christopher is getting rather spoilt as I don't like to let him cry in case he gets on George's nerves. But the milk still flows from its mysterious & inexhaustible source."

When Didy's next baby was born, Elizabeth wrote to congratulate her and described her situation as "char, cook, mother and angry woman." She described her "rather smelly" room and leaky nappy bucket and continued, "Being a woman is really inescapable. We haven't got souls and the best we can be is noble sacrifices. I am not a saintly character at all—I feel homicidal—homicidal but helpless."

Elizabeth had embarked on the impossible: she did not have the income to keep writing and she could not resist having more children. Novelist Fay Weldon met Elizabeth after the war when she herself was a single mother and in her first job in advertising. She said, "I remember going out with her after work. I was unhappily involved with a married man and I was moaning and complaining and she laughed and told me about getting left without money and three children and a fourth on the way and having to get the nuns to help her. Then she said, 'So if you're complaining about a hard time how about that one?'"

I asked Fay Weldon, "Why did women put up with it?"

"It was a time when there was a sense particularly among artistic people that the worse you were to women, the better your Art. Women would get together and compare stories of male awfulness. There was a sense with men's creativity that you had to destroy someone's soul and if you did, it would get into your work. But women believed it too in those days. It was as if the more you responded to Art, the more you believed this. So by being close to the man who was creating, you had a role in Art by proxy."

I started, "But—"

"Life was different then," she interrupted. "In those days men had Art and women had babies."

A MOTHER NEEDS AN INCOME

Shortly after I gave birth to my first daughter, a well-meaning and kindly friend said as I held her, "Now it is time to get your 'self' back." I was deeply engaged with exploring—in mind and body—what it meant to be a mother for the first time. I was trying to integrate this enormous experience into something new. I asked my friend if he would be urging me to get my "self" back if I were deeply preoccupied with a new project in my career.

A century of psychology has articulated love's first paradox, that infants and young children need intense *bonding* in order to become *independent*. Intense bonding is a two-way process that cannot be accomplished by inattentive or depressed parents or caregivers. Intense bonding needs to be attentive and joyful. It transforms into mature love as the child grows into adolescence when young people need adults no less, but in different ways than they did before. We know these things. But we still value identifying with work more readily then we value identifying with child rearing.

Virginia Woolf chose not to have children. It allowed her, in her time and circumstance, to explore her genius. She observed her sister Vanessa with children. She observed Vita Sackville-West with two sons. She admitted a regret at not having her own children. She wrote of Sackville-West, "I like her & being with her; .... There is her maturity and full breast-edness: ... her capacity ... to control silver, servants, chow dogs; her motherhood ... her being in short (what I have never been) a real woman." I find Woolf's remarks both painful and typically acerbic and self-preserving. Her honesty allowed her to construct the original ideas she formulated in *Three Guineas*. Even more radical than her idea that a woman needs a room of her own was her writing that a mother needs an income:

> It seems incredible, yet it seems undeniable ... there is no
> such office as a mother's. The work of an archbishop is
> worth £15,000 a year to the State; the work of a judge is

worth £5,000 a year; the work of a permanent secretary is worth £3,000 a year; the work of an army captain, of a sea captain, of a sergeant of dragoons, of a policeman, of a postman—all these works are worth paying out of the taxes, but wives and mothers and daughters who work all day and every day, without whose work the state would collapse and fall to pieces, without whose work your sons, Sir, would cease to exist, are paid nothing whatever. Can it be possible?

Yes, it can be possible. It was possible when Elizabeth struggled with these issues and it is still possible today. A full-time lower- or middle-class mother cares for her children, cares for the elderly, volunteers at local schools, fundraises, teaches and helps in children's extracurricular events, all on a volunteer basis. Many mothers work full- or part-time at income-generating jobs and do all of this unpaid work too.

Women will never be free and equal until men take emotional responsibility for their domestic lives, until we see men, side by side with women, caring for children and the elderly. Labour has always been measured, consciously, unconsciously or tacitly, by the amount of money one earns in a system that over centuries has refused to acknowledge the labour involved in raising children and tending the elderly. This unpaid domestic labour is therefore unvalued, even by women themselves. A young woman, a successful, high-earning professional, said just a week after the birth of her first child, "I haven't done anything today." We laughingly enumerated how many times she had nursed her baby, cuddled her, smiled at her, talked to her, changed her diaper, all of these acts critical to her baby's survival and well-being. The new mother said, "Oh, you know what I mean. Nothing important."

I long for the day when our culture can sustain the idea that the time and resources required to nurture a child are not a privilege but society's moral responsibility and pleasure. This is a necessity to be fought for with all the passion with which women have fought for a place in politics and at the boardroom table.

PUBLISHED!

Anaïs Nin defied literary taste, wartime gloom and the scorn of her fellow writers. When she could not find a publisher willing to publish *House of Incest*, she bought a printing press. Throughout the Second World War she stood in front of her great press. Imagine the physical effort. Each letter was arranged by hand. Each comma and period and quotation mark. Letter by letter, she set her book. When the press broke down, she learned how to fix it. She lacked the physical strength to operate the press alone so she found a young man to help her. She describes wrestling with the great machine to print her book, which she then sold, copy by copy. She proposed to George Barker, Henry Miller and Lawrence Durrell that they run the press with her collectively, but when the men walked up the six flights of stairs to look at her printing press, when they saw the sheer physical labour and time involved, they quickly wandered back out onto the street. They had publishers willing to publish them. Anaïs Nin did not. During the war, when people lamented paper shortages and small presses closing, when everyone said the sky was falling, Anaïs Nin just kept working.

In Europe, artists struggled to find adequate forms of expression for war, for the civilian bombing, for the holocaust, for the sweeping losses. Marcel Proust wrote, "As people used to live in God, I live in the war." The new war language was about hollow men and madness. In 1944, Francis Bacon painted his *Three Studies for Figures at the Base of a Crucifixion*, grotesque open-mouthed faces with ears but no eyes. Photographer John Deakin shot Dylan Thomas standing up to his waist in leaves in a churchyard. Tony Cronin remembered the pull to the pubs of Soho: "There was a desperation, a poverty. The disorganization of the world was the disorganization of our own lives. I think sometimes we shocked ourselves."

The most colourful poetry magazine in London to survive

the war was *Poetry (London)*, published by a Singalese expatriate named J. Meary Tambimuttu. He was interested in collaboration among the arts, which he called the "circular cine-view." He had a flare for finding talented people. His covers were designed by Henry Moore. He published a Blake-inspired experiment of poetry wound into lithographs, with images by Joan Miró, Max Ernst, Yves Tanguy, Gerald Wilde and Ruthven Todd. He published Mervyn Peake's series of etchings for "The Rime of the Ancient Mariner." He championed Elizabeth's circle of poets—David Wright, John Heath-Stubbs, W.S. Graham, and the triumvirate—Dylan Thomas, George Barker and David Gascoyne. Tambimuttu made the rounds of Soho pubs—the Black Horse, the Burglar's Rest, the Marquis of Granby, the Wheatsheaf, the Beer House—seducing acolytes into paying for his drinks. He said, "A poet is a citizen of the world. All mankind in his principality."

Tambimuttu accepted Elizabeth's manuscript of *By Grand Central Station I Sat Down and Wept* and published 2,000 copies in a slim hardcover in 1945. The cover design by Gerald Wilde is a gorgeous four-colour 1940s design in yellow, red, blue and black. On it, a naked blue woman shaped like a Henry Moore sculpture lies at the foot of the New York skyline, her yellow hair bleeding into buildings. Violent red slashes cut the sky above her. The title is handwritten in small letters at the top and Elizabeth's signature scrawls across a yellow-and-black map of Manhattan at the bottom.

By Grand Central Station I Sat Down and Wept was published a few weeks after the birth of Elizabeth's third child, Sebastian. Though Elizabeth had spent her whole life trying to become a writer, there is almost nothing in her journals about this long-awaited event. She might have been celebrating two joyous moments: a new baby and a first book. But she did not celebrate. She was once again estranged from George Barker, who was sailing back to America to be with Jessica. Elizabeth was alone with a new baby and two toddlers, exhausted and still living on her "dress allowance." She was angry and despairing about her relationship with George Barker. Ten days after Sebastian's birth, just before her book was published, she wrote, "It is unbearable loving George. I always knew he (wouldn't) couldn't come and yet I always expect him and sit in that insane fever of anticipation no matter how I keep telling myself his coming is out of the question .... Suddenly one day I will crack, snap, break into bits and BE GONE."

Elizabeth was rejected once more by her mother for both her third child and her book. No literary critic was ever so fierce as Louie Smart. She burned her copy of *By Grand Central Station*, then bought and burned the six copies available at Murphy Gamble's in Ottawa. She wrote a six-page letter to Elizabeth that began:

> My dear Betty—I did receive your book & have made several
> attempts to write about it. I can't do so without hurting you

& you have hurt yourself so deeply that I cannot bear to add to it. Surely you realize that no mother could not but be shocked & grieved by such a story (I presume you wrote from experience) so I shall say no more about it, only I hope that no more copies will come to this side.

Louie Smart did say more, five pages more. She was hurt at what she called the "none too flattering" view of her and she reminded Elizabeth that she had had more "freedom & fewer restraints than any of your generation." She wrote cruelly:

Thank God your father does not know that you are reduced to living as a char in some man's basement. What he did know completely broke his heart and even admitting it as you once did you could then publish a book to be read widely in Ottawa writing down your father & me & practically holding us up to scorn & revealing the most sordid details of an errotic [sic] "love" episode to complete our sorrow & humiliation ....

Louie Smart allegedly asked Prime Minister Mackenzie King to stop any further copies of *By Grand Central Station I Sat Down and Wept* from coming into Canada. Lists of books banned during the war were destroyed, so it is impossible to verify whether this happened. However, no more copies of Elizabeth's book were imported at that time.

Publicly censored work is often widely read and discussed. It acquires a new value because it challenges the status quo or breaks taboos. If nothing else, people know the titles of banned books. They have heard of *Ulysses* and *Lolita* and *The Satanic Verses*. But *By Grand Central Station I Sat Down and Wept* suffered a fate far worse than official censorship or public condemnation in Canada. It was not discussed. It was not criticized. It was disappeared.

SELF-ABSORBED

In England, the professional reviews of *By Grand Central Station I Sat Down and Wept* were generally appreciative about the prose style, if ambivalent about female experience. The *Times* noted an American obsession with sex while the *Spectator* called it a minor masterpiece. Cyril Connolly reviewed it for *Horizon* and said that both its strength and its weakness was "the magnificent humourlessness of this *Venus tout entière*." He remarked on the author's "genuine gift of poetic imagination, a fine sincerity, and a deep candour in suffering," and ended positively with "... this first book is full of promise and belongs to our time." The *Sunday Times* called the book "exciting and original" and recommended its "sensuous use of language." An anonymous review in the *Times Literary Supplement* praised Elizabeth's "gift for poetic phrase" but stingingly criticized the narrator's self-absorption. This accusation is one that Elizabeth was to hear throughout her writing career.

The recurring topos of "self-absorption" in criticism of women's writing has been lobbed too often at authentic and original voices. I scorn it. I think of Virginia Woolf, Anaïs Nin, Sylvia Plath, and in contemporary times, Anne Carson. I cannot bear to give this critique any consideration at all beyond calling it the clichéd ignorance of hacks. I urge all critics to excise it from their critical vocabularies. It is just another transparent and simple-minded way of trying to make the female "I" disappear.

> "I"

The great originality of *By Grand Central Station* is its use of the first-person voice. The voice belongs to a twentieth-century woman who is ironic and passionate, in love with a married man and pregnant. She knows her literary classics and she has a good ear for the advertising jingles and song lyrics of popular culture. It is a classic romantic love story told from a fresh point of view.

Imagine *Romeo and Juliet* told by Juliet. She might become Rosalind in *As You Like It,* teach Romeo how to tell his love, and turn her tragedy into a romance. Imagine *Tristan and Isolde* told from Isolde's point of view. Or the Persian Layla explaining why she allowed herself to be taken from her lover Majnun. Imagine any of these romantic heroines telling their stories while pregnant. The pregnant female perspective on a romantic love story and adultery was new. There have been few depictions of unmarried, pregnant women in literature.

The narrator of *By Grand Central Station* is no victim. Her pregnancy is part of the continuum of her love affair. She willingly welcomes the husband's betrayal of his wife. She feels no empathy for the husband:

> How can I pity him even though he lies so vulnerable up there in the stinging winds, when every hole that bleeds me was made by a kiss of his? He is beautiful as allegory. He is beautiful as the legend the imagination washes up on the sand.

She quotes his misogyny: "Women have no souls." She acknowledges the betrayed wife's pain and despises her weakness: "This one was the perfect sacrifice .... She was spilt as offering."

The narrator shares the wife's eyes, the eyes of all deserted women. The narrator mourns for lost babies and lost fertility and love's "abandoned and illegitimate children." She calls the baby she carries the "little bastard" and says: "That's the reward of love." She describes women who succumb to love and become mothers: "There is my sister at home with sons for hostage, fighting for one week free to win a job." She describes men's emotional detachment: "... if he saw emotion approaching he smiled painfully, rocking in his swivel chair, hoping it would pass ...." *By Grand Central Station* is a densely described account of the experiences of a female lover, of her sisters, of mothers, of a betrayed wife, of anonymous working girls and married matrons and judging female neighbours. And the men? The father is detached. The husband is singularly absent.

The opening does not describe the lovers' eyes meeting, but the eyes of a wife and a future "mistress" meeting:

> I am standing on a corner in Monterey, waiting for the bus to come in, and all the muscles of my will are holding my terror to face the moment I most desire. Apprehension and the summer afternoon keep drying my lips, prepared at ten-minute intervals all through the five-hour wait.
>
> But then it is her eyes that come forward ....

A psychological brilliance is the revelation of the "love

object" as unworthy. A fumbling, shuffling husband appears from behind his wife:

> Behind her he for whom I have waited so long, who has stalked so unbearably through my nightly dreams, fumbles with the tickets and bags, and shuffles up to the next event which too much anticipation had fingered to shreds.

Later, his touch makes the narrator ashamed of being a woman:

> One day along the path he brushed my breast in passing, and I thought, Does this efflorescence offend him? And I went into the redwoods brooding and blushing with rage, to be stamped so obviously with femininity, and liable to humiliation worse than Venus' with Adonis, purely by reason of my accidental but flaunting sex.

The first words the husband speaks are uttered "as impersonally as a radio discussion" and they are not about her, but about a homosexual tryst:

> ... he tells me, "A boy with green eyes and long lashes, whom I had never seen before, took me into the back of a printshop and made love to me ...."

The first physical description of the husband's face is a reflection in a car window, "merciless as a mathematician," and the narrator experiences his first kiss on her forehead "like the sword of Damocles."

Let's recap. The husband shuffles, fumbles, talks impersonally, has a merciless face, makes his lover ashamed of being a woman, and talks about a boy-lover. The only conventional thing about this romantic hero is his kiss of death.

After a long description of the wife, the narrator describes herself and the husband as mythically transformed. For this she uses conventional love-language:

> I am the land, and he is the face upon the waters. He is the moon upon the tides, the dew, the rain, all seeds and all the honey of love. My bones are crushed like the bamboo-trees. I am the earth the plants grow through. But when they sprout I also will be a god.

Although the lovers are arrested at the Arizona border, the narrator continues to live her passion both for itself and as self-exploration, intercutting her personal reflections with language inspired by the Song of Solomon in the King James translation of the Bible:

> Take away what is supposed to be enviable: the silver brushes with my name, the long gown, the car, the

hundred suitors, poise in a restaurant—I am still richer than the greediest heart could conceive, able to pour my overflowing benevolence over even the tight mouthed look. Take everything I have, or could have, or anything the world could offer, I am still empress of a new-found land, that neither Columbus nor Cortez could have equaled, even in their instigating dreams.

Set me as a seal upon thine heart, as a seal upon thine arm, for love is strong as death.

But the husband's feelings for her are wrapped in violence and rage and misogyny:

Remember also, when you hold your so vulnerable head between your hands, that what we are being punished for, and worse, what we are punishing for, is not just the sea of peace we achieve when you call me You Bitch, but the Cause. (The cause, my soul.)

... Do you see me then as the too-successful one, like a colossus whose smug thighs rise obliviously out of sorrow? Or as the detestable all-female, who grabs and devours, invulnerable with greed?

Alas, these thoughts are your sins, your garments of shame, and not the blond-sapling boys' with blue eye-shadow leaning amorously towards you in the printshop.

The betrayed wife regrets her abortion and rages against her husband and the narrator: "One day she said, Then have your orgy with Blondie, work out your passion on her."

The love affair is now on its downward spiral. The husband prefers to read his newspaper, and openly hates his lover:

Here is the bed where love so often liberated us and dissolved the walls, but where also the night shook him by the collar like a dog till he spat out the rag ends of his fear: "You're a cunt! You're nothing but a cunt!"

In the end, the narrator is left alone, pregnant, listening to New York's vivid street talk: "Sure, kid. We all got troubles. Buck up. Take it on the chin."

Passion has not destroyed her. Passion has transformed her:

Then I speed through Grand Central Station with nothing at all to stop me, like a careering limousine without brakes, propelled by my brilliant desperation.

It gives me talent. It manipulates the small terrorizers of before. I storm them with scorn.

The narrator does not die for love, like Juliet or Isolde or Anna Karenina. She survives to tell her version of the story in her own voice. She finds her "talent" and a scornful strength. She was the agent of all the action, her love affair is the means to her transformation. She will soon be a mother. The first word in the book is "I." The last words in the book are "Do you hear *me* where you sleep?"

ALL FEMALE

After the publication of By *Grand Central Station*, Elizabeth got pregnant for the fourth and last time.

One of the universal mysteries is the desire to bear a child. It is irrational. It is unmediated. It is visceral. Elizabeth was fascinated by the power of nature in her own body during her child-bearing years. She wrote of childbirth as a profane form of spirituality in *The Assumption of the Rogues and Rascals:*

> Useless to invoke God then. He stands awkwardly aside like a husband at a birth, and nature like a red-cheeked midwife flounces flamboyantly round.
>
> Will you let this rough woman have command, God? Will you leave me to her mercy as she puts dust-sheets over my eyes and folds my mind away? He will. He does.
>
> I try to remember how, when birth comes, the dams will break, and God will assume His majesty and roll in

pain like an avenger over my drenched soul, and love and
blood flow back into the world.

I have heard women speak of "finally understanding" during
childbirth. They say, "So this is what it is all about," without
naming either birth's primal power or its whiff of death.

To some extent birth just is. I like Margaret Atwood's
description in her story "Giving Birth": "Birth isn't something that has been given to her, nor has she taken it. It was
just something that has happened so they could greet each
other like this."

Birth is also an experience of lived extremity. My own
memory of giving birth is of how time and space disappeared
at the end of my labour. I was the still centre; there was nothing but pain and breath. The threshold between life and death
receded. The helping voices and tending hands around me
seemed disembodied and remote. Through my own body I
was both instrument and agent of nature. It is clear to me
why certain women want to have many babies and why many
women take new directions after childbirth.

After the publication of *By Grand Central Station*,
Elizabeth moved to Markham Square in London and kept an
open house for artists. They called it the Poet's Kitchen and
nicknamed Elizabeth "Sat Down and Wept." Nicolette Davis
remembered "her beautiful sad face and her air of awaiting
disaster with a saint's resignation." She wrote that at

Elizabeth's "... people were so important that all work must stop, that time must be made and the milk could boil over for the sake of words exchanged in communication."

Elizabeth planned to move the family to Ireland where life would be cheaper. Her fluctuating dress allowance had been reduced after her father's death and she had no other source of income. Once again, she was heading to a place where she knew no one, in order to have a baby. She wrote to Didy, "We're having another baby in February. George said before he left it doesn't matter how many children we have now."

Elizabeth and George could not sustain what they were living. Life outside the romantic archetype crashed in: babies, George's wife and other lovers and children, the need to write, the need for enough money to buy milk. Elizabeth later said wryly, "He really only loved me two weeks or two months."

Elizabeth's letters to Didy Asquith at this time are a study in trying to create a new paradigm. She had broken with all social convention and assured herself a perverse kind of freedom from its restraints. Not only did she have an appetite for children, but also she had an appetite to write experimental prose. She struggled with what she wanted to achieve in her work from her earliest diaries to months before her death. In 1938, she wrote what remained true to the end: "... the oblique camouflaged form of putting the truth in a work of art. A Poem, a note, a diary. These are the raw moments, the raw thoughts. I do not want, I am irritated with the devious method and hidden indirectness of the novel, for instance, or even the short story, or a play. Poems, notes, diaries, letters, or prose such as 'The House of Incest' or 'The Black Book' only meet my need."

She remained unwaveringly true to her aesthetic. At various times throughout her life she toyed with working in more conventional genres. She noted down ideas for films, a biography of Marie Stopes who was a pioneer of birth control, thoughts about a plot-driven novel. She did publish a cookbook. But as she wrote to painter Stephen Amor in the seventies, "... I have to follow faithfully my own peculiar way, a nameless, unidentifiable, uncategorisable, idiosyncratic way."

Even in her final journals she searched for a name for her writing. Only three years before her death she wrote: "I knew, always knew that I am not a novelist, never was, never wanted to be. So why do the niggling markings of people who don't understand what I am lurk unhelpfully around, getting in the way. Just because there's no NAME for it?"

She is referring to her prose style, but her themes were also unfamiliar. We have had stories of adultery in Western literary tradition since the Greeks and Romans, since Chaucer, since Dante. But we have not had stories of women who *keep* getting pregnant while unmarried and *keep* loving their children's father. Elizabeth stayed connected with Barker in various ways—as a former lover, as her children's father, and latterly, side by side with him as an artist. She wrote about her experience as an artist living alone with her children.

I think that the process of living this new plot began—painfully—in Ireland. It was the year Elizabeth grew most desperate. It was the year that she kept no journal.

A NEW PLOT

"It's odd how you came just now. I was just going to throw these letters away," said Didy Asquith as she handed me a large envelope of letters from Ireland.

That night I was exhausted by the emotion I had felt everywhere when people talked about Elizabeth. As I lay on the bed, my mother, who was travelling and researching with me, began to read the letters. The room fell still with the silence of someone absorbed. I watched her face deciphering the difficult script, observed her familiar expression of empathy, then saw a small furrow of pain declare itself on her clear brow.

"It's so sad," she said after a while.

"What is?"

"She was so alone. Even when he was there. She'd just had a baby and could hardly feed the other three."

"She said she loved him."

"Hmm."

"Why hmm?'

"I don't think a woman ever forgets how desperate she feels when she knows she might not be able to feed her children."

⁓

On the west coast of Ireland, little thatch houses with tiny windows huddle against the wind. Rough stone fences cut crazy enclosures for dirty sheep that press up against the stone for shelter from driving rains. The roads are narrow and the bus driver honks his horn continually to warn animals and carts around hairpin turns in the road. West off the main road, the bus climbs into rougher and wilder hills, through prickly thistles and purple heather and yellow buttercups. Near the coast is the smell of the thick bottom of the sea where tides leave the ocean's flotsam naked on the sand. I could see the Virgin Mary everywhere, in stone grottos beside the road, above cottage doors, in front of churches, her hands stretched out open and waiting.

Elizabeth arrived in Roundstone (Cloch na Ron) in November 1945 with three children. She rented a house called Hillcrest on the main street. Along the road was Connolly's Bar where Harp lager is squeezed out of green porcelain taps. Hillcrest has two big front rooms, a kitchen downstairs and four large bedrooms upstairs with gables and salt-caked windows looking out to sea. The drafty stone building was

I'm so happy with Rose — &
everything, including my figure, is
returning to normal much faster
than usual. Lots of people came
to call & brought presents, & I now
feel there are some friendly
souls around — it was horrible
feeling the hostility before.
The hate, or whatever it is in George's
soul, is a very dangerous chemical—
He really did Paris a while village.
          I sent a postcard at Rose's
birth addressed to "Barker" —
but nobody has written — not
even the usual congratulatory line
from Big Mumma — no word
from Kit or Wendy since they left.
I wonder what the situation is, but
I don't much care. I've learnt
to smoke professionally, & have at
last made up properly that
piece of real silk you gave me
2 years ago — also a bit of
a linen bureau cover you gave me,
& a bit of white linen someone gave
me here. I love it — it gives me

33

. my sense of security.
I've decided to earn my living
selling them to Bond Street shops
as exclusive designs —
It's real sweating now — I can't
believe I can do it.

Sue never refers to her
baby coming — except that she
mentioned Erik Reed was her
doctor. Doesn't she like to
talk about it? I don't like
to unless she does. Have you
seen Rene? Poor Donald has his
exams in about ten days, I think.
I hope everything is alright.
Having babies from birth to 2 weeks
is so heavenly — I can see now
why I keep weakening.
Wish that state could last —
maybe I can keep it this time.
IF

heated with tiny stoves that burned peat and dung. Through the back garden, up a few stone steps, is a Protestant church. All summer and autumn brilliant red fuchsia grow on the hedges. Small children like to rub the centre of the honeysuckle bells on their palms and lick off the sweetness.

I walked up the single street of Cloch na Ron and asked the old women if they remembered Elizabeth. It was that kind of place—small enough that people will remember what happened there three or four decades earlier. No one in the post office knew a thing but in the pub memories were longer. After I bought a couple of rounds, a few voices at the bar spoke up:

"Yes, she had a baby here."

"There was an English husband."

"Some kind o' artist."

"Sure, him and his brother came all dressed in black."

An old man sitting at the bar put his cap on and tipped it down over one eye rakishly. He grinned and said, "He wore his hat like this! And we called them The Gangsters!"

Everyone laughed and drank up. Those were the details remembered after forty years—the nationality, the tip of the hat.

By the time I left the pub, most of the village knew why I was there. I went to Wood's Dry Goods store next door to Hillcrest. I asked a middle-aged man behind the counter whether he knew anyone who might have known Elizabeth Smart or Elizabeth Barker.

He smiled. "I've been waitin' for you. My mother's back here, Brigid Woods. She tried to help take care of her."

He led me to an old woman sitting beside a stove. She said, "Elizabeth was a lovely girl. She used to run up and down those steps to fetch a bit of bread or lard for the children. John made her a cradle of red deal and she painted it lovely with a long vine and green leaves along the side."

The painted cradle was passed from woman to woman and into poetry. Therese Cronin rocked her youngest child in it and George Barker immortalized it in a verse from his "True Confession" that begins, "I sent a daughter to my love/In a painted cradle."

Brigid Woods recalled in a gentle lilt, "She was so pleased with that cradle that John made her a little table for the children too and she painted a great cross through the middle of it and wrote each child's name on it, one on each side with a blank spot for the baby. She was always kind and oh she was lovely with those children. We felt a bit sorry for her all alone. My husband John gave her milk from our cow. He took her up to the top of the village to a dance and she danced all night, long after he was tired. She was longin' to hear Irish music but she couldn't get out much."

By the end of the first month in Ireland Elizabeth was unable to pay the rent. It was the most desperate period of her life. Her letters are marked with characteristic little half-moon cuts she made with her thumbnail as she read and wrote. She had met some Dublin artists and had arranged to go into the city to meet Leslie Daiken, who praised *By Grand Central Station* as surpassing Auden and Spender. But she cancelled her meeting with him because George Barker telegraphed that he was coming. She was wrangling with Barker over money and Jessica and their twins, and she wrote to Didy: "... I don't know whether this isn't the moment to give up a luxury I cannot afford either financially or emotionally. All he'll ever be is a lover when he feels like it—& now the bed's so crowded with ghosts that there's not really room to make love."

Elizabeth's mother had remarried and built a new wing on The Barge at Kingsmere to take in two British war children as well as her eldest daughter Helen's two children. She offered to try to help Elizabeth settle in a small town near Ottawa. She exchanged angry letters with Elizabeth when she discovered that she was pregnant again, and Elizabeth wrote to Didy that if she moved back to Canada and her mother's help she would have to live a "pure virtuous life, according to Canadian matrons' standards—I don't think fresh orange juice is really worth THAT, do you?"

By this time George Barker was living part time in London with Cass Humble, a woman with whom he would spend the next decade, off and on. Elizabeth wrote to Didy that she was "very near madness of the undefined type," that she did nothing but masses of mending. She could not get along with the villagers who she thought were cheating her. The photographs of her in Ireland are very uncharacteristic. She looks emaciated and she is wearing a gold cross around her neck. She mailed a letter to George Barker in late December trying to break off their affair: "Relationship can't be romantic when there's always another contemporary passion going on. What remains—& it does remain, is a rock of Gibraltar starkness that stands anything except the indignity & the degradation of petty deceit."

George wrote back that he was too old for "romantic" attachment and that it was impossible to feel romantic about a woman whose only successful affair was with herself. Once again we hear the recurring criticism of a woman for self-absorption. A woman, in art and in life, was not to be self-absorbed. Even if she had written a book. Even if she was feeding her children on nettles.

Elizabeth wrote: "Dearest Didy, ... I feel rather irritable and very lazy .... The simple life DOES require a simple complement such as old fashioned marriage .... Maybe after I get rested, I'll be a female novelist & Buddha."

That year, Elizabeth could never get enough milk for the children. She had a housekeeper for a while but couldn't pay her. She was constantly out of candles and food. She took care of her family on one pound a week.

The struggle between Elizabeth and George took on a new cruelty in Ireland. He and his brother Kit arrived for a month's visit in December. George found Elizabeth's home claustrophobic. There was no money for candles and they spent their evenings in the dark. Elizabeth wrote to Didy: "As for Love, it's OVER—As for sex, it's revolting—As for cosiness, it's no longer cosy—As for desire IT HAS FAILED."

The brothers ran up bills in pubs and stores until the entire village cut off their credit. Then they went to neighbouring Galway and did the same thing. They told an old shoemaker that Elizabeth would pay for new soles for their shoes when her money came from America. Elizabeth wrote to Didy: "... I loathe George now & I am absolutely cured of him forever—he has been revolting all this time that we were eating potatoes & the little people were knocking on the door with their bills. He & Kit spent (I discovered last night) £40 this last month in the pubs here—while refusing to pay a single bill—or even give cash for food—& then complaining like mad at the lack of it—& it isn't as if they'd even been jolly or gay—just abject & selfish ... he spent all my monthly allowance in London & my family Allowance & won't pay anything back but gets furious if I mention money or bills. Thank goodness at last the pubs refused also to give credit or cash cheques—but now he's got a store in Galway to send stuff & cigarettes and will *never* pay them. And if there are 4 chops for 8 people he eats 2 whole ones—Jessica sent him a letter last week, too, saying she's been hounded by debt collections & George has spent about £150 on *nothing* not even any fun. He's been *poverty-stricken* the whole time.

It's definitely cured me—"

Barker left when the BBC wired him money for his fare, and Elizabeth wrote to Didy, "He really did *Panic* a whole village." She finished, "It isn't that I want him to support us but only not to take what we have."

Elizabeth had once written that she would "repopulate the world." As her last child began to shift toward the world, she shifted with it. She grew buoyant and thought of names. She wrote a will, as she did at each birth. And just before the birth she scribbled ferociously, "A fig for Romantic love."

Her journal account of the delivery was more detailed than for any of the other children. At a time when many women were delivering their babies anaesthetized, Elizabeth knew exactly what was happening to her body and her baby.

> Show about 8 am very mild pains at intervals all morning. Nurse came about 1, doctor examined me & left. Enema about 3 (no shaving). Pains still mild. Began to get uncomfortable about 3:30. Was given an injection of pituterin to speed up pains at about 20 to 4 & in 5 minutes pains got very severe & came one after another till the bearing down ones of which there were only 3—one opened bowels, one brought head right down & third head was born, followed by body at 4:03 ... doctor arrived after birth & removed placenta. After pains were stronger & oftener than usual, but general reintegration was quicker than usual. She was

bathed by nurse & end [umbilical cord] tied & put in cradle. I was especially shivery. I gave her glucose & water from a silver spoon at 10 pm & she settled down for the night with hardly a murmur. I didn't sleep but dozed towards morning & fed her about 7. She learnt to suck easily. The nurse came to bath her & we borrowed scales from Miss Curly's shop and weighed her. There were only big weights & she weighed more than the 9 lb one—& not as much as 1/4 lb package of glucose I had—roughly 9 lb 23.

The children were thrilled with her ....

Who took care of the children? Who helped Elizabeth during those first weeks after the birth when she would have been nursing every three or four hours? She still had three children under age six who needed tending. She wrote that she was never so peaceful as after the birth of each of her children. She described her "arch-angelic" postnatal state to Didy: "It's wonderful the way youth & vitality & sanity & possibility & initiative RETURN after a baby—it's so strange to feel things again—almost to venture out again. Don't forget this if you feel dead & defeated by circumstances …."

She was terribly alone. There was no mother or sister or friend to help. There were words, always her solace, words. She described to Didy the great feeling she experienced after giving birth: "… if I go for a drive with the rector, or go to church (I did on Sunday) or have *anything* inside happen, I can't stop huge oceanic subterranean emotions about age-old things coming over me, and if I'm left alone (away from home) I cry."

She scrawled big messy words across the centre of her letters:

Do you know, I love Rose so much I almost long for a 5th—
Isn't Mother Nature Awful & Cunning but anyhow she's
my friend.

After the birth of Rose, Elizabeth tried to give up George, but she still wrote to Didy for news of him and then chastised herself: "It makes me mad that I should still be so interested …

DAMN HELL & DAMNATION. If only the rich duke would come galloping by begging for my hand & the 4 pairs of hands which are included with it .... It is hopeless quite quite hopeless although I AM MARRIED to him & I love him."

She chose the word *married*, the only word strong enough to express what she felt about her relationship with Barker. But in Ireland Elizabeth had begun to invent the life that she would live, a life without conventional support or marriage or even her own writing. She was living a story she could not yet write. Men would come along who were willing to play the role of the rich duke, but Elizabeth never accepted. On the grey coast of Ireland, she played oracle and muse to herself: "... the truth is that I am broken-hearted (fatally wounded) quite literally but I look forward to friends and cosy conversation & a pretty place to live & being admired & having people drop in & the children being successful in all spheres they attempt. There's no solution with George possible .... What I want is a social life (not necessarily brilliant or high) with lots of other peoples' problems & troubles to worry over."

The heaviest weight of love was to be the sweet child who murmured in her arms through those long Irish nights. When the children were asleep she made smocked dresses for her daughters. She made miniature books of George Barker's poetry. She made lists in her journals. Elizabeth could not write, but she found solace and joy in her new baby and in the fleshless embrace of language.

LISTS

Nearly all the women writers I know keep lists in their heads of other women who write. I've talked to women painters and musicians who do this. Women in politics and in the corporate world do it too. Women professors don't make lists of women professors any more but take careful note of women who head departments or become university presidents. Women doctors and lawyers make lists of women surgeons and women judges.

Women pull these lists out of their heads when they are passed over for a promotion at work or when they fight with their partner over domestic responsibilities. They pull these lists out of their heads when they decide *not* to go further in their work. Some women refine their lists by creating a subdirectory of "women with children who work." They rage, fight some more, then put the lists aside with a laugh or a grumble depending on their dispositions.

Elizabeth loved lists. She kept lots of them: for plant identification, for possible husbands, for her babies' early accomplishments, for her writing. Here is one she kept revising throughout her life:

> Women Who Wrote
> Sappho
> Jane Austen
> Emily Brontë
> Charlotte Brontë & Anne
> Christina Rossetti
> Ivy Compton Burnett
> Emily Dickinson
> Stevie Smith
> Baroness Blixen [Isak Dinesen/Karen Blixen Museet]
> Colette
> Mme de Sévigné
> Djuna Barnes
> Margery Kempe
> St. Theresa
> George Eliot
> George Sand
> Marianne Moore
> Barbara Comyns
> Kathleen Sully
> Fanny Burney
> Jane Carlyle
> Dorothy Wordsworth

Caitlin Thomas

V. Sackville West

Virginia Woolf

E. Nisbet

Louisa M. Alcott

Anna Sewell

Harriet Beecher Stowe

Kate Douglas Wiggin

Elizabeth Bowen

Kay Boyle

Hannah Arendt

Mrs. Eliz. Gaskell

Edith Wharton

Willa Cather

Katherine Mansfield

Margy Webb [perhaps Margaret Alice Webb]

Johanna Spyri

Selma Lagerlof

Mrs. J. Ewing

Mary Louisa Molesworth

Mary Lamb (with Charles)

Mary Russell Mitford

Mrs. Craik [perhaps Dinah Maria Mulock Craik]

Maria Edgeworth

Mrs. Ann Radcliffe

Mary Shelley

Agatha Christie

Margery Allingham

Ngaio Marsh

Elizabeth Fenors [sic]

Muriel Spark

Iris Murdoch

Doris Lessing

Mary Wollstonecraft

Joanna Southcott

Mrs. Bate Eddy

Marie Stopes

Harriet Martineau

Simone Weil

Jane Taylor

Harriette Wilson

Mrs. H. More

Leslie Blanch

Anne Rider

Audrey Beecham

Carson McCullers

Mary McCarthy

Simone de Beauvoir

Diana Doss [sic]

Jean Howard

Julie Strachey

Alma Karan [sic]

Fran. Mallet-Joris

Fran Sapan [sic]

N. Mitford

L. Riding

Eudora Welty

Anaïs Nin

Edith Sitwell

Anne Finch, Countess of Winchilsea

Anne Bradstreet

Anna Freud

Dorothy Parker

Margaret Kennedy

Susanna Moodie

Gypsy Rose Lee

This list, dashed off in a diary, reveals the marvellous breadth and taste in Elizabeth's reading. Not only was she thoroughly conversant with contemporary prose and poetry, but in a time well before "women's studies" she had read the lesser known writers from the medieval period forward. She read such non-fiction as Webb's *Bibliography of Canadiana* (1940) and Jean Howard's accounts of being a Hollywood hostess. She includes Jane Taylor's critical work on the French poet Villon, and covers a full range of genres, including children's literature. And this was only her list of women.

There is an unsated appetite for these lists. Louise

Erdrich's list in *The Blue Jay's Dance* (1995) emphasizes
women with children who write. Erdrich begins her list of
forty-three women "and many, many others": "I collect these
women in my heart and often shuffle through the little I
know of their experiences to find the toughness of spirit to
deal with mine." Carolyn Heilbrun creates many short lists
in *Writing a Woman's Life* (1988) and remarks, "Women
come to writing, I believe, simultaneously with self-creation."
In some cases this self-creation includes having a child, in
some cases not. Such lists may provide us with enough good
reading to fill many a snowy night. They give us life models
and show us what women have done before, where the sacrifices have been made. But we also need to look forward. We
need invention, new ways to think about work and creativity
and raising our children. New stories out of the old.

INVENTING A LIFE

The children and Elizabeth are thin in the photographs from
Ireland. Elizabeth is always turned towards one of them, a grace-
ful hand reaching to one or another child, the other arm cradling
the baby. She could not earn a living in Ireland. They were

hungry. Elizabeth's sister Jane wrote to say that she had found a place called Tilty Mill where Elizabeth could live near London.

Tilty Mill is an old miller's house at the twelfth-century Abbey of Tilty between Dunmow and Thaxted. The monks drained the marshy land around the abbey and put down waterworks for milling and fish preservation. Later they introduced sheep farming. Their sister abbey was Tintern in Monmouthshire, where William Wordsworth reflected on the "still, sad music of humanity." What remains today of Tilty, after the ravages of the English reformation, is the old gate and a church with a magnificent east window, a towering arch over a stone-carved mandala of the Holy Trinity. The church is called St. Mary the Virgin.

Elizabeth was depleted. She moved the children to Tilty, then wrote to Didy that she was going to London to stay with Michael Asquith's cousin, Sue Boothby, at Sussex Square: "I must get away from myself & my children for a while ... I have such awful dreams."

Sue Boothby had vivid memories of Elizabeth's warmth on her visits: "I had a friend, Antoine Bibesco, who knew Proust and who lived on the Ile St-Louis in Paris. He decorated his apartment walls with gold and silver to reflect the waters of the Seine. He would walk in the door and see Elizabeth's coat hanging there and bury his face in it and sigh, 'Ah, sublime Betty!' He loved to go on long walks and talk with her." Even depleted and desperate, Elizabeth was at ease in any circle.

She settled at Tilty Mill from 1948 to 1954, and tried different work and living arrangements with the children. She was still living on a reduced dress allowance from home. She hired an Irish nanny for a very short time. She invited Michael Wickham, the photographer whom she had met before the war in the group travelling to Cassis. He came to their home to photograph the children for magazine fashion spreads and he became Elizabeth's lover, working part-time in London and living discreetly with Elizabeth at Tilty Mill. Elizabeth began to write freelance articles for *House & Garden* magazine. She and Michael entertained friends—photographers, artists, editors—Cedric Morris, Kingsley Martin, Julian and Ursula Trevelyan, George and Pat Haslam. On one boating excursion at King's Head, Landermere, Elizabeth sailed the inlet toward the sea with publisher James MacGibbon and Michael Wickham. On the way back, battling wind and tide, their boat got stuck in a narrow channel. They anchored and the men looked from one salting to another for a way back without getting wet. As if she expected to walk on the water, Elizabeth stepped right over the edge. James MacGibbon recalled, "Betty looked very maritime in her blue jersey and trousers and Michael was particularly elegant, breast-stroking the sixty yards across the channel, pipe in mouth, hat on head." This was the Elizabeth everyone loved to remember, the woman who found spontaneous and playful solutions to life's exigencies, the woman who stepped out over the edge.

Wickham's black-and-white photographs provide a peep into life at Tilty: close-ups of the children, of Sebastian grinding Elizabeth's coffee, of Rose in her crib reaching toward her mother, of Georgina and Christopher playing outside near the millpond. There are shots of Fred Barltop the miller standing near the pump which he started each day with his legendary 400 pumps, and of Madge Girdlestone sitting at the table with a cup of tea after her long walk up the Tilty track with the post. There are shots of Elizabeth on unmade beds, of her sitting smoking at the uncleared table in the clutter of a busy household. There are exotic shots of her standing with feathers in her hair in front of a voodoo doll. There is a series of shots of Elizabeth on a trip to Paris. She is wearing a hat decorated with a wide ribbon and a double-breasted jacket. She looks girlish, sitting in the car of a merry-go-round, standing in front of an outdoor doll stand, walking across the wide green lawn of the Tuileries.

Louie Smart visited Elizabeth once at Tilty. It was the first time they had seen each other since Russel Smart's death, since Louie's remarriage, since the publication of *By Grand Central Station I Sat Down and Wept*, and since the births of Elizabeth's last three children. I try to imagine what it would have been like. Elizabeth had defied every social convention and she still could not imagine herself free of her mother's judgement. According to Michael Wickham, Elizabeth was "terrified of her mother." He said he was "tidied up" and sent away to London. He laughed at the memory: "No fucking, we might get caught. Weird, really, looking back. Her relationship with her mother was difficult. Elizabeth wanted to fix things up."

I liked listening to Michael Wickham talk about his affection for Elizabeth after all those years. His eyes softened and grew bright at his memories of her. His conversation revealed the same layered quality as his photographs. Just under the surface of flat domestic detail—dirty cups, rumpled sheets, a crib's chipped paint—lay an intense emotional life. His memories and pictures caught Elizabeth's fascination for small children in a kiss with baby Rose. They also caught her frustration and the sheer labour of her life in her already work-worn hands. They caught a valued intellectual life in books lying open everywhere. They caught the growing addictions in full ashtrays and empty glasses.

Michael Wickham shared his pleasure in the memory of this affair and couldn't help some boyish boasting as he remembered conspiratorial lovemaking on his Bechstein grand piano. I appreciated his candid admission of regret for this lost love. He said that although he had loved Elizabeth, she had never really loved him. After about two years with Michael, she broke off the relationship by letter while he was away in France on a photographic trip.

At the end of our talk he saw me off at the train with an enormous bouquet of flowers that he called a tussy-mussy, one of each flower blooming in his large garden. Later, he sent a letter with memories of Elizabeth: "There was some pain at the end .... Betty was always jolly good company, witty and fanciful and wonderful in bed!"

It seemed odd to me that he didn't know she had been writing then. When I asked him, he replied, "I don't believe she wrote anything at that time. If she did I never saw it. Secretive always."

"But what did she do on your trip to Paris?"

"Well, I painted and took photographs. I don't really remember what she did. I think she shopped."

But she did write. Though she wrote nothing about Michael Wickham and remarkably little about her children, she was writing the first drafts of *The Assumption of the Rogues*

and Rascals: about post-war gloom and post-childbirth struggles and building a life built on redemptive suffering.

After she sent Michael Wickham away, Elizabeth had to find
new child-care solutions that would allow her to work more in
London. In 1950, when Rose was three and a half, Elizabeth
sent all four children to Pinewood School in Hertfordshire as
weekly boarders. But the arrangement did not work out. She
found it painful to be separated from the children and was not
satisfied with the school. Besides, Rose was too young to be
away. Elizabeth moved the family briefly into London at the
end of the year, but because of difficulties with her lease she
returned to Tilty in 1951. She then put the children in the local

school. She invited two of George's friends, the Scottish painters Robert Collquhoun and Robert MacBryde, to live at Tilty. The eccentric, hard-drinking Roberts took care of the children during the week so that Elizabeth could work in London. She came back on the weekends.

She kept sparse diaries during those years. She expressed a fierce frustration at her inability to write. Her diaries only sketch in a few complaints and list names of the guests from London who came to her weekend parties, but the children remember more detail. They remember fights and dancing, broken furniture and windows. The children remember pushing their beds together in the bedroom upstairs for comfort. Elizabeth's diaries do not record how she did laundry for a household of five (or more) by hand or how she learned to iron with a hot spoon. They do not record that the nearest food shop was several kilometres away and she had no transportation. Her diaries omit how no one helped her on those weekend visits, and they do not mention the occasion when she broke every dish in the sink and went running out the door. Georgina recalled these things and Christopher Barker has written a short account of his memories of Tilty in which he characterizes the adults who visited as the "wild bunch that peoples my childhood nightmares." He describes the alternating tenderness and cruel jokes of his caretakers. Robert MacBryde cajoled and joked and sang with the children. But MacBryde was also capable of baking a stone into the centre of a meringue and tempting his trusting charge to bite down. Colquhoun came into the house from the painting studio at tea time and gathered the children round the table to happily compete at drawing a perfect circle. But when he came home late at night from The Rising Sun pub, he terrified the children sleeping upstairs by slamming doors and breaking glasses and shouting at MacBryde, "... I'll faaackin' *keel* ye!"

At that time, Elizabeth was not seen as a writer by anyone in her circles. She was seen as the mother of four children and as *one* of George Barker's lovers. There was no writing community that included her. Many of the poets and painters whom she invited with their various girlfriends each weekend openly argued that women could not produce art. Elizabeth scrawled her objections in big penciled words, scribbles of rage, across her journal pages and chastised herself for not speaking up. Once, after everyone left, she wrote: "Everyone wanders around not knowing what to do, worrying about money & about not being able to work. I'm writing all this because I'm in the same condition. Huge bills, a great wasting of days. Nobody getting any pleasure *or* good, just waiting for time to pass. Robert does some housework. So do I because I think I have to, or they'll [the children] be disgusted in their hearts. The children's ears and necks are filthy & their hair is matted & dusty. I don't care. I don't care who says slut either. It's too much."

I think that Elizabeth stopped her creative writing because she was exhausted. I also think that what she wanted to write seemed too dangerous. I think that the raw pain of feeling abandoned with her children and not being able to write so filled her with rage that she feared writing anything longer than terse diary entries. The inferiority of a woman artist was an idea so cruelly dominant, so culturally accepted, and so frequently voiced in her circles, that she may have had a difficult time feeling worthy enough even to articulate her objections. But whether she had the nerve or the time for it, she still felt compelled to write. Even years later she wrote of this period, "I always felt guilty not writing."

When Elizabeth was a young, single woman in Canada, financially supported by her family and secure in her social position, she could turn cartwheels on Parliament Hill and read poetry from the trees. But in post-war England she lived with men considered the best artists of their generation who actively denied her artistic accomplishment. They did not acknowledge her published book. They prevented her from developing artistically by eating the food she needed for her children as they drunkenly told her that women can't create.

Yet she kept inviting them to come. This is the point in Elizabeth's story at which it becomes difficult to understand why she allowed these men to continue getting in her way. Without more of her reflections on the subject, we cannot know. We do know that she was always hoping that George, the father of her children, would be among the weekend guests. Perhaps she was subject to the feeling that women shared men's art by proxy.

Elizabeth's Tilty Mill diaries are punctuated by desperation, her handwriting large and looped and angry: "Love. Children. Earning a living. Friends. Drinking. Pushed too far to do too much. Silent years. Desperate from hating."

She struggles to keep writing. She scrawls desperately across the pages:

WRITE, JUST DO ANYHOW.

She had written something in 1944 that remained true all through those Tilty years: "I realize that I am afraid to say the important things and therefore there seems little point in this book except as an exercise in description and daily domestic details. Perhaps one thing will lead to another—or the truth will emerge from the omissions."

What did she omit? What was concealed?

THE GIRL VOICE

Jenny Mortimer visited on those wild weekends and experienced refuge and self-discovery with Elizabeth. She said, "It was all because of Elizabeth that I realized I had a voice at all." Jenny had run away with a photographer and the first time they visited Tilty Mill, someone threw a plate of spaghetti through a window. Jenny recalled feeling intimidated by the artists and trying to sit quietly so she wouldn't be noticed. When Robert MacBryde was told to tone down his talk in front of such a nice girl, he got up and stood directly over her.

Jenny said, "He bent down close to my face and said gruffly, 'Being nice is not enough.'" She laughed. "I suppose he was right."

She described with deep affection how Elizabeth warmed up the rooms by covering the walls with crinkly brown parcel paper. She described Elizabeth's love for the children and how she thought it was exotic to live with the two Roberts. She recalled how Elizabeth encouraged her.

Jenny said, "I felt that I didn't dare open my mouth in front of all the men. One night Elizabeth said to me, 'You have a lovely voice, Jenny. You must sing.' No one had ever told me I could sing before. I couldn't do it, but another night Elizabeth asked me again." She told me about her terror and her pleasure. She sang a few bars for me as if she were still sitting in that twelfth-century miller's house:

> My man he rocks me, with one steady roll.
> My man he rocks me, he wants daddy's hole.
> The clock strike one
> I said, Daddy, now ain't we having fun
> And he went on rockin', with one steady roll.

The Roberts joined in that night. Jenny told me it was the first time she had been brave enough to sing "in front of all the men." It was Elizabeth who helped her do it.

THE MOTHER VOICE

Mothers' diaries are still a mostly unexplored genre of journal writing. I think of the immense detail of Virginia Woolf's
journals recording her intellectual and social life, and of
Anaïs Nin's voluminous diaries detailing her psychological
world. Yet, I have seen few diaries recording the dailiness of
being with a child. Elizabeth did not keep them, though she
kept detailed records about certain other parts of her life.

I have experimented with documenting my own daily life
with babies and toddlers. Reading the journals afterwards is
like looking at waves upon the shore, each wave different, and
yet in its entirety, a vast sea of rhythms and continuities, punctuated by memorable storms and occasional doldrums. Moods
shift from one instant to the next. Fleeting moments become
the source of the most profound joy and connectedness. Small
epiphanies erupt in the necessary routine of domestic life; a
small child's unfolding imagination and confidence emerge
with her daily independence. Any given hour may seem eter-
nally slow. Yet at the end of a week, or a decade, time seems to

have evaporated. There are moments of tending small children that are filled with such frustration that one is ashamed to record the harsh words, the startled look on the child's face, the slammed door, the guilt. There are long days of harmony and companionship and pleasure that nourish and sustain.

Life begins in the animal moment of birth, a state of fierce concentration out of chronological time. The first weeks and months of nursing every few hours are also outside of any usual cycle of day and night. Gradually a mother (or caregiver) helps her baby sort out day and night and then begins what we lightly call *socialization*. It is a word I do not like. I prefer to call the first six years a time of guiding children toward their independence, both in and out of community. It is a time of allowing them to explore their inner, imaginative life. It is about being there to support and provide guidance but also about keeping out of the way. It is about trusting in, fostering and sharing a quiet joy in individual growth.

Both writing and mothering take place in a time that is outside the world of government and law, the world of commercial trade and such daily social service as teaching and medicine. That does not make them less legitimate. All are necessary and none needs prevail over the others, but traditionally the spheres of both nurturing and uncommercial creativity have been firmly kept to the margins. Why?

In my journals, I see my own growth as a woman as I observe my children's developing characters. I have recorded the nature of our days together, the quotidian repetition that flows over the rich interior life, getting dressed, having breakfast, what was said, getting out the door, what was seen. I have stood at the edge of their play and listened to their monologues and to their play talk describing their experiences and feelings and inner worlds. During one such monologue one of them noticed me and turned and said, "Don't listen, but don't go away." She was working away at the greatest task of childhood—imagining and then acting out her independence. I have written down the words from play, the long stream of their confidences and fears and lovewords as they were falling asleep at night, my husband's and my most impatient words spoken in moments of sleepless desperation, our shared pleasures and our transformed love as parents. I have written about the moments of plain old fun being together, of the golden light of a late summer twilight illuminating the faces of my two daughters out on a boat on a northern lake. I have described the heavy, dreamless sleep just before dawn when it all begins again for another day. I have described how my own mother, who stayed home with her children full time and who rarely gave advice, insisted poignantly, "Be sure you keep working. They will grow up and go. Keep something for yourself too."

Writers make clear decisions about how much to reveal of friends, relatives, acquaintances, children. What is a betrayal of their relationships? Each writer must decide. Adrienne Rich

wrote anecdotes about her life with her sons in *Of Woman
Born* that have saved me in my own mothering. Louise Erdrich
has caught the fierceness and sensual beauty of life with a
baby in her diary of a birth year, *The Blue Jay's Dance*. Both
women have been honest about themselves. But both women
have protected their children with respect and tact. Erdrich
created a combination of her three babies for her book and
asked her readers to forgive any "obliqueness" in her descriptions because, "After all, these words will one day add to our
daughters' memories, which are really theirs alone."

Elizabeth did not write what was essentially her great
experiment in child rearing. She tried many different child-
care solutions—staying at home, babysitters, nurseries, live-
in help, local schools, boarding schools. Not all her
experiments were successful. In her very unconventional life,
one of the few ways in which Elizabeth was conventional was
in her choices about education for her children. She wanted
an academic education for her sons. She sent the two boys to
The King's School, Canterbury for a traditional Anglican
public school education. She sent her daughters to Legat, a
non-academic Russian ballet school. Georgina later spent a
year at the Sorbonne to learn French; Rose tried a variety of
alternative educational programs, including an unsuccessful
year at High Mowing School in Wilton, New Hampshire, in
the United States, when Elizabeth had hepatitis. When Rose
returned to London, she had private tutors. She left home the

following summer at age sixteen, involved in a love affair that would prove destructive. Rose did not thrive on the lack of convention in her upbringing and education. Everyone who knew her spoke of her beauty and intelligence, her intensity and wit, but she was unable to complete her education or find a relationship in which she could develop. She would become addicted to heroin and spend time in drug rehabilitation programmes at Spellthorne St. Mary in London. She was to have three children. A friend who wished to remain anonymous said with great empathy for both mother and daughter, "Rose wanted something solid under her, but Elizabeth was unable to give it." It is important to remember that Rose's father was absent.

Elizabeth experienced years of trial and error and effort while raising her children. I suspect she had many insights about child rearing, but she wrote very little about them in her diaries. She did write a little in her later poetry about her remorse over Rose and about trying to combine mothering with art, and she was very conscious of her relationships with her children when she was trying to write about her own mother in her later journals. But when Elizabeth's children were still young, she only wrote: "I realize that I am afraid to say the important things."

SOHO

Elizabeth had a personal typology of drink. She referred to the "little drink" as a quick, social drink with no possibility of intoxication and without consequence. She was more interested in the "big drink," by which she meant the momentary transcendence between sobriety and drunkenness. She described the "big drink" as the place where discoveries can be made, a place where protective barriers are shed, a portal into bacchanalian revelation.

When I went to Soho I visited The Colony Room, one of Elizabeth's favourite haunts, a private club that, at the time of my visit, was presided over by Ian Board. I climbed the stairs and crossed the threshold into a world where ambition, achievement and credentials are scorned. Ian Board, with one stiff leg, sat on a bar stool at the end of the bar. He greeted everyone by name, praised their clothes and made fun of their work. I went with M. (a pseudonym), who nodded at Ian Board and said conspiratorially to me, "Did you ever see a nose like that?"

The walls of The Colony Room were covered with aging black-and-white photographs and the cash register had no cover.

"We only put the cover on on Sundays," said Ian.

"Or when royalty comes," said someone at the bar.

"Fuck, it never had a cover."

"Doesn't matter, it's ruined most of us."

M. got up and brushed past Ian Board, repeating loudly, "Did you ever see a nose like that?"

"Are you talking about his face or his ass?" said someone at a nearby table.

"His face."

"His best asset."

Raw-throated laughter. Cigarette smoke. More drinks.

"Is Liz a great favourite in Canada?" a man at the bar asked me.

"Yes, she has lots of Canadian readers."

"All thirteen of them?"

"The rest of us just drink," I said. "Have a drink?"

More laughter and mocking North American plumbing and tales of how much Elizabeth hated Canada.

"When Liz came back she said, 'I knew there was a reason I escaped.'"

M. pulls me away. "My mum was never around. I was raised by nannies so I ran away when my mum married again. I met Elizabeth at Tilty when I was seventeen. She had these four children. She'd just feed them all and talk the whole time and pack them upstairs to bed. I loved her. I admired her. I wanted to have a baby. My mum was big on powder and lipstick but it was Elizabeth who taught me to be a lady. I loved seeing her with Rose."

The afternoon spins on. Someone stumbles and Ian Board says kindly, "Rough seas? Decks rolling?"

A glass gets knocked over and someone else says, "Welcome to Soho."

"Open arms and legs."

They talked about the old days and recited poetry. Their greatest tribute to Elizabeth was repeated over and over that afternoon: "Liz was a real Soho person."

When I left The Colony Room that night, a drunk in the shadows outside on the sidewalk startled me, and I turned, frightened. But he only said, "God bless you." I took a taxi home and fell into bed. I lay there wondering how to describe the atmosphere of the place. What one reads about Soho always seems flat compared to its extraordinary ambience. Photographs tell even less. That night I dreamed that there was a tribe of little dwarves gathered around my knees swaying and chanting, "Bliss, bliss, bliss." I laughed myself awake. The power of the bacchanalian remains more ineffable than most things. In Soho, its power can be both destructive and transforming.

Muriel Belcher ran The Colony Room in Elizabeth's time. Over a thirty-year tenure, she turned running her club into an art form. Elizabeth called The Colony "womb-like" and wrote about Muriel's particular genius, saying she was a "nanny who dispensed rude words like soothing hot milk."

Elizabeth wrote a tribute to her after her death: "... she made you feel safe. And you didn't have to be a homosexual or a black or a battered love-object or drunk to appreciate the protection that her high camp aura cast, though she did make homosexuals feel gay long before they started bandying that useful little word about.

"She was brilliant at relaxing shy people. 'Meet Sun,' she might say to some respectable inhibited elderly homosexual man. 'She's had more pricks than you've had hot dinners.'

"That broke the ice."

Why private clubs? Why did a place to drink need to be womblike?

Women's social segregation is neatly revealed in bar habits—*where* they enter, *where* they sit or stand. In Canada in the 1950s, women who went to bars (if they went at all) were required to enter through a "Women and Escorts" door and to sit in restricted areas of the room. This charming custom prevailed in many places for several decades. In England in the 1950s, women could walk alone through the door of the pub but they did not go up to the bar. Their drinks were passed back through the crowd and their money passed forward. Elizabeth said in a Canadian interview, "The London pubs were great places for literary activity. Everyone gathered at the various places to talk and drink. Women sort of kept back on the edge of the crowd as the men discussed all the exciting things that were happening."

After Dylan Thomas died, George Barker held court alone in Soho. The atmosphere after the war was so charged that people who could not, or did not want to, rejoin "ordinary" life stayed in Soho. They said they had "sohoitis." People recall how George Barker created an atmosphere of sexuality and charm and extremity with his poetry. People talked about sweeping his poems up off the floor at closing time. The other artists in his circle, David Wright, Patrick Swift and Tony Cronin, stood listening and talking nearby. Therese Cronin said that the women were separated from the men, and often from each other. She said, "They'd make sure that Cass Humble [a lover of George's] was standing at the far end of the circle from Elizabeth, with Kathryn Malloney and Pip Wright and me in between. 'St. George' we used to call him among ourselves."

The men in Elizabeth's circles knew her very little, although after the pubs closed they went regularly to her home to drink and eat and sleep. The poet John Heath-Stubbs said, "Pubs were a man's scene. Women, if they went, were sort of prostitutes or lesbians. They hung around the back. It was just part of the British mentality at the time. I didn't really know Elizabeth. I was more a friend of George Barker's." David

Wright knew Elizabeth better in the later years, but of the 1950s when he frequently stayed at her home, he said, "I'm afraid I didn't get to know Elizabeth at all in the early years." Editor Martin Green wrote candidly, "I first became aware of her as a dimension of George Barker."

Women found a much more inclusive and welcoming world in such private clubs as The Colony Room, with its unconventional and campy atmosphere. Elizabeth was a great favourite at Muriel's. Margaret Fenton remembered meeting her there, "You know, women may spend their days worrying about a child's drawing without a sun, but these things were rarely spoken of in the pubs. Elizabeth was the only person in Soho that I talked with about my four children. Women just stood around the edges. No one talked to them. But Elizabeth never minded talking about anything."

THE SILENT YEARS

Elizabeth moved from Tilty Mill to a flat in London at Westbourne Terrace in 1955. By this time the children were in boarding schools and came home only for holidays. Although Elizabeth called these her "silent years," at her busiest she was churning out copy for three different jobs at once to make the kind of living that can maintain a flat in London and keep four children in school. During the 1960s, she was said to be the highest paid copywriter in London. She also allowed her flat to be used by a wide circle of poets and writers and artists. Poet Patrick Swift and his wife Oonagh lived in the basement. When Robert Colquhoun died suddenly of a stroke, Robert MacBryde moved into a tiny extra room in Westbourne Terrace. His loud and drunken mourning inspired the children to dub it "the wailing room." George Barker too visited and stayed for short periods.

Patrick Swift and David Wright launched a literary magazine called *X* (1959 to 1961) from Elizabeth's Westbourne Terrace living room. Elizabeth wrote a promotional slogan for the magazine, "Would you buy a brandy for Baudelaire?" which was rejected by the editors. It must have been painful for Elizabeth, who was writing in her journals that she was "desperate" to do her own creative writing, that the editors did not invite her to contribute to the magazine. Yet she continued to provide them with a place to meet, with food and drink. She still helped to type up the interviews. Therese Cronin described Elizabeth's selfless hospitality in this way: "There are givers and takers in life. Elizabeth was a giver. Sometimes people took advantage of her. But it was the only way she could be."

Tony Cronin said that Elizabeth wasn't seen as a writer. "George overshadowed her. She only wrote one book and it came about because of him so she was left in the shadow of her own creation." Martin Green recalled an occasion when George and Elizabeth were downstairs in poet Patrick Swift's flat: "It had been mooted unkindly by someone that she had never written anything worthwhile herself. She pointed out that she had written *By Grand Central Station I Sat Down and Wept*. But George said dismissively, 'I gave you the title for it.'"

Two world wars had set women back. In London in the 1950s, there was still rationing; times were pinched and conservative when Elizabeth began to work in journalism. In one of her first magazine articles, "The Artful Art" for *Junior Miss*, Elizabeth wrote advice to young girls on how to make conversation with a man: "The first thing you have to learn is that your own thoughts are the very last things to be communicated. You can never have your say. You must find your satisfaction in letting men have theirs. Don't let the rewards of the suffragettes, or elegantly dressed women executives, or Joan of Arc, or a beautiful female politician bamboozle you into error. They probably won their point by leaving it unstated, or else they're the sort of lonely lady you don't want to be. 'God preserve us from clever women,' say all the clever men."

Elizabeth may have been writing for her market but she had learned these sentiments young. When she was still a girl she had visited J.M. Barrie, her favourite childhood author, armed with an introduction from a family friend. She asked him whether or not women should be educated and afterwards wrote in her journal: "He said he admired anyone who wanted an education and didn't think it spoilt anyone. He thought girls that went [to university] were better to talk to. He said, 'But a clever woman never lets on she is clever. Whenever you hear anyone say 'That woman is clever' you know that she is stupid. A clever woman doesn't let you know."

Elizabeth spent a lifetime fighting this deeply sown message. In later life she dealt with it using irony and wit. At her granddaughter Claudia's wedding, shortly before she died, Elizabeth sat down next to George Barker and drawled campily, "George, do you think it is a disadvantage for a woman to be clever?"

Several drafts of her first magazine articles remark that an equal education may not be "attractive" in a woman. One of these pieces is titled "Can Women Be Educated?" Elizabeth wrote, "He wants a beautiful and intelligent wife but the fact that she has passed through college and has a number of letters after her name does not interest him to any great extent."

But she very quickly left such preoccupations behind and became a first-rate features writer and copywriter. She had abundant ideas and speed. Maria Kroll, a former *House & Garden* editor, recalled her professionalism. If she didn't always get to the office in time, she wrote amusing excuses in the sign-in book and she never missed a deadline. Sue Boothby said: "She was busy raising these four children and writing and she'd sit with me and say, 'I suppose people will think I'm making a blow for single mothers, but I'm not. I always say, get him to marry you. I couldn't get George to marry me.'" She was working because she had to and she turned her pen to money-making copy.

Tom Woolsey, who worked in advertising with Elizabeth, said that she achieved an unusual intimacy in her copy because she always wrote from her own experience, as if she were writing to one person. In this way, even her fashion copy felt universal. He said, "She could look at the shape of the ad and write just the right number of characters. I always needed a grain of sand to work against, but Elizabeth didn't. She just came in, took off her jacket and started in."

I asked, "When you were working with her, there were problems at home and she had four children in various boarding schools. She was trying to figure out the best way to bring them up and still write. She must have been very tough."

He said, "'Tough' is not the right word. Perhaps it is more 'self-sufficient.' She once said to me, 'If you've read Proust you'll never be shocked.' Well, I've read Proust and I'm still shocked. But she had that kind of culture. She was not shocked by anything."

"Did you ever go with her to Soho?"

"Sometimes. I found Soho like no other place I've been. They were direct and cruel to each other, witty and kind, all at the same time."

"What do you mean?"

"I suppose you could say it was because all those people had been through an awful lot. There was nothing to hide. They'd seen all the warts. Elizabeth had this openness to life, to all experience. She lived life in the round. Her work was as important as other things, but not more or less. With some people you knock up against a wall, but Elizabeth didn't have any walls."

Elizabeth was perfectly suited to the emerging sixties in London; she rejected class distinctions and embraced free-spirited living. She joined Crawford's ad agency in 1953, where she worked until 1966. The offices were located in an art deco building at 233 High Holborn, a quick walk to Soho, so that she could move easily between the high-paced world of advertising and the timeless bohemia of Muriel's or The Coach and Horses. The people she drank with didn't know, or didn't care, that she was one of the hottest ad writers in London. She juggled ad writing at Crawford's, and later at Graham & Gillies, with copywriting and fashion spreads for *Man About Town*, the *Tatler*, and later *Queen*. She also wrote freelance features and interviews. She was prodigiously productive.

The child who had been a fierce mimic of Ottawa society tea talk was now a middle-aged woman transforming her own children's slang into advertising copy. I was fascinated as I talked with people who worked in Elizabeth's advertising circles. Thirty years later, these people ran some of London's top advertising companies and still spoke of her work with nothing short of reverence.

"She was the best writer I ever worked with."

"She seemed to have a computer in her head. She could give you exactly the right number of characters to fit a column."

"She was a divine presence. She was a great pleasure and very malicious and incredibly fast."

"I'd give my grandmother to find another writer like Liz."

One of her biggest compliments came from the master himself of 1960s advertising, David Ogilvy, author of *Confessions of an Advertising Man*. Elizabeth reviewed his book and played on his famous Mercedes slogan "At $50,000 the loudest noise you'll hear in this car is the radio." She titled her review, "At £22,000,000 yearly turnover level, the loudest noise in advertising is this quiet cocky Scot." After the review appeared, Elizabeth received a telegram from him in New York asking her to come and work for him. He liked her style.

London's top sixties model, Twiggy, brilliantly parodied the prim closed knees of the wartime fashion world, although her kohled eyes and pigeon-toed stance were more reminiscent of dancers in Stravinsky's *Rite of Spring*. London photographers such as Terry Donavan and Bill Klein and Norman Parkinson moved out of the studios and onto locations. Their pictures began to run with such captions as 'Youngest, happiest, going-est'—and the words were frequently Elizabeth's. She was the first writer to get away with using the word *sexy* on a fashion ad. People were pushing language and social limits toward new informalities, and Elizabeth easily combined language from "high" and "pop" culture, just as she had in *By Grand Central Station*. She made allusions to *Oedipus Rex* on a shoot in front of the pyramids, and she wrote on a Jaeger sweater ad for men, "A cashmere cardigan by JAEGER brings out your sybaritic potential to its uttermost."

Vernon Stratton, then an advertising director, said, "She was on top of the trends. She was the first person I ever heard use the word 'mini-skirt.' Once she had to go away for several weeks and I couldn't get anyone to do the work right. When she came back in, I said, 'Liz, see if you can do anything with this.' She had it in ten minutes. She was incredibly fast."

Andrew McCall described her work on the Jaeger campaigns: "Tom Wolsey and Vernon Stratton had formed a new company. I was an assistant. It was my job to be barman and make sure there were enough cigarettes. Liz moved among the models, looked at the scamp [first] layout and sat down in front of a typewriter to begin work. I used to hand her measured ad paper but she just grabbed any scrap and wrote. The atmosphere was always very fraught. Deadlines. Late at night. Once Vernon didn't like an ad Elizabeth and Tom were preparing and he picked up the whole thing and threw it out the window. All their copy went fluttering down to the ground, and he said, 'I can't work with you anymore!' I'd drive her home after work and everyone would congregate at her house. In the early sixties there was a narrowing of the age gap and Elizabeth was right into that. She brought people of all ages together. Fashion was a young people's business and Elizabeth could bridge all those groups. She always made me feel at home."

Dennis Hackett, editor of *Queen* magazine at the time, said, "She was very, very good. We talked a lot about writing. She could handle anything. We often used to go out for lunch. She'd say that I reminded her of her father. There were never-ending crises with the children and Barker. Sometimes it all got too much. There was an atavistic feeling to her. My office had a glass wall so I could see her come back in her cups [tipsy] after lunch. Once she came in and rang me and said, 'I resign,' and I answered, 'You're fired.' In a little while my door opened and Elizabeth was down on all fours crawling in, then I saw her hands on my desk and she stood there in front of me for the longest time and sank down again and went back to work."

Perhaps she did want to resign. But she still had her children to support. She could not write. When she drank her frustrations sometimes came out. Yet, her closest friends and her family consistently remember that she was not self-pitying, even drunk, and that she "just kept going." Elizabeth herself described the conflict she experienced between her need for solitude to write and her need to make a living and be with people: "Melancholy and despondency .... I never did say one needs nobody *ever*. But how to arrange it so that they don't take all and that some stimulus comes from outside without destroying everything."

Elizabeth succumbed to her arduous work and social pace and fell ill with hepatitis in 1961. She spent nearly a year mostly in bed, working from home, helped by Hase and Michael Asquith. She stopped drinking and smoking for a time. Her diaries list many friends and family members dropping in. Throughout her recovery she still supported her children and continued her copywriting from Westbourne Terrace. She did no sustained creative writing but she was always thinking about it. As she slowly recovered from hepatitis she noted images that she planned to rework in *The Assumption of the Rogues and Rascals*. In a big messy scrawl she covered her diary pages with shorthand notes like this:

Love
    An idea
J C's
    Tenable?

In the 1960s there was growing affluence and recovery from the war. For young women, there was the birth control pill; there were better opportunities for education. Women's emancipation movements were stirring up once more, and bras would soon be burning. Penelope Hall recalled her first job at *Queen:* "I was young, down from Oxford, and I was a

KIM ECHLIN

secretary and I couldn't type. I adored Elizabeth because she was kind to me. She took me to lunch at these places in Soho. I had a crush on her, for her gifts, her passion, her belief in Art with a capital *A*. The magazine was hip, flashy, sophisticated, with lots of superficial values, but Elizabeth appreciated what was good. She was very discriminating. We loved her bohemian life, how she'd thrown up her life for her lover and had children without a husband. There was a huge glamour around her bohemianism. She wrote very witty copy. She transformed the stick-in-the-mud fashion copy to writing that really reflected people out doing things."

But one woman (who did not wish to be named) recalled a more private side. She said, "Elizabeth felt she gave away all her strength to other people. When she was drunk she'd say, 'I have this gift that I'm not using.' It was like looking at an open wound. I found it paralyzing."

Young women were slowly learning how to speak up again. Fiona Green told a story from the 1960s that I heard in many variations: "I had been running around making heaps of food for a party and topping up glasses. The room was smoky. There were always readings at the parties and George Barker pulled out a book and began to read, then Colin McInnes did too. I said, 'I'd like to read something.'

"Someone said, 'Baby, bring me a drink.' It was so humiliating. Finally, a younger man said, 'I'd like to hear you read.' I did read, but the silence was awful."

Elizabeth's way of speaking up had always been writing. She had learned to survive by writing what she could not say aloud. Irony and wit gave her a measure of protection from the despair of feeling silenced. Of the dozens and dozens of "Elizabeth ads" I saw, my favourite is a Bill Klein photograph in which a young Jaeger model leans on the nude thigh of a relief sculpture of a man. The skinny pigeon-toed model looks straight into the lens, one finger held up to her lips, coy and secretive. She is wearing a straight dress with a scalloped hem and a lace-trimmed neckline. Elizabeth has written across the genitals of the sculpture: *Be Straight Laced!*

SPEAKING UP

My own adult life begins to overlap with this period of Elizabeth's and I want to emphasize for a moment the cultural atmosphere in which Elizabeth was writing. Her 1970s book reviews brought back lots of memories.

1972: I was a teenager writing poetry. A boy told me I shouldn't put the word *cunt* in my poem because it wasn't "very nice," although he used the full palette of language in his own writing. It wasn't supposed to be nice.

1980s: I was an undergraduate and graduate student, working part time in journalism. I warded off persistent sexual advances in a newspaper job and by a professor at different times. I was a television producer at the Canadian Broadcasting Corporation when Anita Hill decided to press sexual harassment charges against Judge Clarence Thomas. The day the story broke, my female colleagues throughout the office suddenly admitted their own stories of sexual harassment at school and in the workplace. That amazing day in the office was the first time in my life that my female colleagues "told."

1990: I was pregnant. A literary agent said to me, "Put away your writing. Enjoy your new baby." I asked him if he stopped working when his children were born. He said, "Oh no, but it's not the same."

1991: I was a new mother. I approached my employers with a practical scheme to job-share with another mother. I was refused outright by an executive who also happened to be a new father. He said, "There are lots of ways of managing full-time work." I asked him how he was managing. He said without a trace of embarrassment or irony, "My wife is at home."

2002: I was at home caring for my second child. I had just published my second novel. I was working freelance, teaching and editing. (There is still no national daycare plan.) I was working on a translation from Sumerian and writing this book. I wrote in the early morning hours before everyone else got up. A man stood in the doorway of my own home and said to me, "You're out of things. You lose perspective when you're out of the workforce."

2002: In a discussion comparing Carol Shields' *Unless* with other books on a literary prize list, a *publisher* said, "That book will not win anything. It is too much a *woman's* book." Anne Carson's writing is accused in a print review of being "self-absorbed."

These experiences are not walking to town to cast your first vote because your husband refused to let you use the horses. Time falls away. We get on with things. But imagine the effect on the women of the thirties and forties and fifties of repeatedly hearing that women should hide their intelligence, that pregnant women shouldn't work, that women don't need an income. Elizabeth chided herself frequently in her journals, "Can't I possibly be a bit braver?"

My own mother negotiated her way through roughly the same years as Elizabeth did, though she was raised in a less permissive and privileged social milieu. I asked her why *she* thought Elizabeth stopped her creative writing during the years when she was raising her children. Without an instant's hesitation my mother answered, "Too much resistance."

Elizabeth first publicly articulated her ideas about women writers in a fortnightly book review column for *Queen* magazine. She wrote from a well-stocked mind in an intimate, conversational voice. She reviewed the latest literary fiction and also wrote about books that had "weathered the silent years." She brought wide literary and life experience to her columns:

June 30, 1965

How does one convey the goodness or badness or inbetweenness of a book? Good of its kind? That's all very well for books on flower-arranging, or generals' memories, or prostitution, or concentration camps, or cookbooks. But would it work for *Alice in Wonderland* or *The Anatomy of Melancholy* or *A Sentimental Journey*? If it's *very* good, it's not like anything else. When this dilemma faces me in the course of my reviewing duties, I ask myself where I would place a book in my own library, which is a very idiosyncratic, but strict and sometimes insulting, arrangement of books which I am always changing to amuse myself, rather on the hostess's principle of seeking piquant juxtapositions. I like to try out fraternizations that might amuse those involved: *Seven Types of Ambiguity* with *Robinson Crusoe*; Saki with Plato; Hazlitt with George Herbert; Horace with Beddoes; Congreve with Scott Fitzgerald; Cardinal Newman with Cervantes. All with an equally suitable companion on their other side. The women, departing from the hostess principle, I have segregated. I did this in a fit of pique one day, having listened week after week, until it was the last straw, to men, mostly Irishmen, declaring that women were incapable of creating works of art.

She was interested in the difficulties faced by women artists. She was formulating a way of reading women's literature separately yet with equivalent literary standards. In a column called "Girls Who Write," she began: "A lot of men I knew kept saying that girls can't write. Or paint. Or whatever. This got on my nerves, eventually. So I have segregated the ladies from the gentlemen in my bookshelves."

In her *Queen* book review columns, she finally had a forum in which to discuss her views on literature, unhampered by dismissive conversational remarks. Her writing in these columns was cultivated and witty and intimately drawn from her own experience:

September 8, 1965

Sometimes I look out of the window and people look disgustingly half-finished. Sometimes I look out and they look rich and lovable. Yet they're the same people each time—just people passing. How they appear depends on whether I'm loving their humanity or hating them for not being more god-like. With books it's the same, rather more so than usual this fortnight, but tending towards the fraily human rather than the godly. There's nothing I'd steal for, or die for, or fight for; nothing that's a reproof or an inspiration; but a lot that's admirable, and some things that are highly diverting.

Elizabeth championed good style. In this column she listed as literary forebears Sappho, St. Theresa, Marjorie Kempe (forerunner of Simone de Beauvoir, Joanna Southcott, Marie Stopes, Mrs. Eddy), and worried about such "overlooked sisters" as Georgina Rossetti and Dorothy Wordsworth. Only the best, she wrote, "stand alone" and among these she included Jane Austen, Ivy Compton Burnett, Colette, Virginia Woolf, the Brontës, Djuna Barnes, Stevie Smith. She noted the prejudices against women writers and worried, perhaps ironically, perhaps not, about speaking up:

Any day, of course, you can observe men pleasuring themselves with Agatha Christie, Nancy Mitford, Dorothy Parker, Harriet B. Stowe, Kate Douglas Wiggin, Louisa M.

Alcott, Leslie Blanch, Marjorie Allingham, Ngaio Marsh, and so on. But I get the impression they think that what these ladies write is just an advanced, though delicious, form of *petit point*. Not serious stuff. A further, darker thought, is that it is in no lady's interest to speak.

Then she speculated about the possibility of women writers working in a different voice. In spite of such writers as Marianna Moore, Mme. de Sévigné, Fanny Burney, Anne Bradstreet, Barbara Comyns, Caitlin Thomas and Baroness Blixen, she notes that some women writers "talk a different language." These she called the "cleverer girls" and listed among them Iris Murdoch, Gypsy Rose Lee, Dame Edith Sitwell, Hannah Arendt, Simone Weil, Anaïs Nin, Françoise Sagan and Mary Shelley. Then she reviewed new books by Brigid Brophy, Doris Lessing and Sylvia Clayton. This short column is Elizabeth's first public stab at tackling "women's literature." She managed to throw in the names of forty-five women writers, affirm a female writer's voice and object to different critical standards for male and female writers: "... it's not sporting to wince when they're [women writers] too direct, or to insist that they refrain from speaking *their* truth."

She pointed out that, after so much neglect, women writers must be *read* and *discussed*, which was difficult when so many of their books were out of print. She did not mention that her own book had been out of print for twenty years.

"I DON'T THINK THAT *BY GRAND CENTRAL STATION* IS ROMANTIC"

Attitudes change. In 1966, Panther Books published a paperback edition of *By Grand Central Station I Sat Down and Wept*. The book was resurrected and gradually discovered by a new generation of women who were interested in the unconventional love story and its powerful narrator. The book was well reviewed, but it still had a cult reputation more than a general one. No one had asked Elizabeth in 1945 what *By Grand Central Station I Sat Down and Wept* was about; they did when the book was finally reissued in 1966. After a quarter century, Elizabeth said that her book was about exigency: "... I don't think that *By Grand Central Station* is romantic. I would obstreperously deny that it is romantic. It *is* realistic. You get into a state where you fall in love and I'm not saying it was a good or bad state, but I just wanted to describe how it was, and I think I did that."

Interviewers asked the inevitable question: Why hadn't she written more? Elizabeth answered tartly that she'd been

Each woman was trying to free her own children from the restrictions she herself found unbearable. The restrictions were manifest in the *personal* mothers, but they originated in the culture. The Baldwin-Smart-Barker daughters needed, as any daughter does, their mothers' help to become independent, to have a firm sense of being loved, to stand up to whatever restrained them in society. The daughters of each successive generation need their mothers' help to continue discovering their freedom.

Rose Barker died of liver complications sixteen years later, at age thirty-six, a mother of three. Elizabeth was devastated by the loss. After Rose's death she wrote: "So the pain sits still, crouching, heavy, occupying all my inside, always, all the time, whatever my outside does ... she suffered, cried for help, suffered, & still loved on. Was bewildered, found it too painful. Died. Where, if anywhere, do a mother's responsibilities end?"

OF POETRY AND GARDENS

It is not romantic to raise and support four children alone and to try to keep a creative life alive. Although a few women manage to earn a living, raise children, and keep their creative lives going, it is very, very difficult to keep three balls in the air. In 1966, at The Dell, taking care of Rose's children, Elizabeth was once again facing the difficulty of trying to do her own writing in a busy domestic situation. This became the subject of some of her later prose and poetry, but years would pass before she could get it down on paper.

She did not want to write in short, disciplined snatches as one often does with small children. She had never worked creatively this way. She did not want to write in two- or three-hour bits. She wanted time and she wanted to "go deep." She found that she could not write, so she created a garden.

I like the descriptions of the legendary garden that Elizabeth created out of an acre of clinker at The Dell. Beth Chatto, who also carved a garden and a nursery business out of the inhospitable Suffolk soil, described Elizabeth's home: "It was a 'Secret Garden.' You couldn't see out the windows when you were inside and there was a wonderful green gloom over the cottage. You lifted shrub branches laden with flowers to get round a corner. You moved vines and found little paths, places where tiny things move. Walking through it was like opening the pages of a book. It was beautiful in a dishevelled magical kind of way. It was not a hit or miss garden. She'd planned it and then let it look after itself. We are such creatures to prune and clip and tidy. I can't afford, in my own mind, to let my garden get like Elizabeth's. I find it magical to be in a place where plants can be themselves.

You have to have courage to make a garden like that."

Elizabeth was less romantic: "I gardened furiously because I couldn't really write with those tiny children."

She named all the parts of her garden: the Magic Circle, the Heather Hill, the South Point, the Azalea Bowl, the Poet's Corner. Near the gas house was a small shed she called the Summer Palace. Vines grew between the chinks in the walls and into the mattress on the rough stone floor. A favourite spot was the Bear Garden to which Elizabeth led her grandchildren on processions with offerings. One year, there was a pond that her son Christopher helped build. There was a willow grove, and gold heart ivy growing over the kitchen window. It was both a plantsman's and a gardener's garden; it was a four-season garden and a wild place. She planted sweet honeysuckle and lilac for their perfume near her door. She had six types of peonies and different kinds of clematis climbing through the elders. Perfumed philadelphus and Jerusalem artichokes were set in the sun and in the shade. Garlic popped up around the dwarf fruit trees—apricots and peaches. She made swatches of colour along the gravel drive with spirea, forsythia, flowering almonds and lilacs. Gentler pansies, sweet Williams, forget-me-nots and lily of the valley grew close to the house. Tall sunflowers drooped at the height of midsummer. In July, there were red poppies and opium poppies with pink and mauve blossoms. Each fall she planted more and more bulbs. The last fall before her death, she planted 2,250 bulbs—hyacinths and daffodils and narcissus and tulips and crocus and allium and muscari and lilium and scilla.

She collected Canadian trees and wildflowers—trillium and birch. There were things to eat—rhubarb, asparagus, leeks, artichokes and herbs. There were lots of fungi, which she cooked and served to dubious guests, saying, "There are only a few kinds that can kill you. The rest will only make you sick."

Some of Elizabeth's oldest friends were gardeners—Hetta Empson, Isabel Rawsthorne, David Carr. She liked to visit John Morely, a painter and a plantsman in Suffolk. He described with fondness their lively plant-buying excursions. At the end of the afternoon I asked him why he gardened. He paused for a moment and answered wryly, "Well, I suppose it's so I don't have to paint."

Elizabeth marvelled in her diary at the pleasure of watching Rose's daughters grow. Twenty years before, in an article called "Good Living" for *House & Garden* she had written: "Anyone with creative or useful work to do may get it [good living] from that, but there is an even better source—children. The ancient procreative truths ... cannot be left out of an inventory of the needs of good living, even if there is a risk of revolting the sybarite ...."

The best of Elizabeth's late poems deepen these reflections. She refused to privilege one form of creativity over another. She wrote using a simple lyric line and plain diction:

The Muse: His & Hers

His pampered Muse
Knew no veto.
Hers lived
In a female ghetto.

When his Muse cried
he replied
Loud and clear
Yes! Yes! I'm waiting here.

Her Muse screamed
But children louder.
Then which strength
Made her prouder?

Neither. Either
Pushed and shoved
With the strength of the loved
And the unloved,

Clashed, rebuked:
All was wrong.
(Can you put opposites
Into a song?)

In this same long poem Elizabeth looks back to other literary woman, all childless:

> Stevie, the Emilys
> Mrs. Woolf
> By-passed the womb
> And kept the Self.

> But she said, "Try
> And see if it's true
> (And without cheating)
> My Muse can do."

> Can women do?
> Can women make?
> When the womb rests
> Animus awake?

Vanessa Bell called maternal love "... one of the worst of the passions, animal and remorseless. But how can one avoid yielding to those instincts if one happens to have them?" Virginia Woolf said that being a mother can "kill the one who devotes her life to it." Anaïs Nin linked what she called the maternal instinct to masochism: "A mother ... suffers, gives, feeds. A woman is taught not to think of herself, to be selfless, to serve, help. This masochism is almost natural to woman ...."

I think there are (necessary) confusions in all of these observations. There is confusion of instinct with social conditioning, of instinct with passion, of necessity with desire. But successive generations pull apart the inter-twined threads, each a little differently. There seems to be no single way of articulating the conflicting desires a mother experiences.

A painter such as Kaethe Kollwitz did not experience her mothering as limiting, though her father had warned her ominously when she married that it would be impossible to combine domestic life with her art. She wrote years later: "I am gradually approaching the period in my life when work comes first. When both the boys went away for Easter, I hardly did anything but work. Worked, slept, ate and went for short walks. But above all I worked. And yet I wonder whether the 'blessing' is not missing from such work ... formerly, in my so wretchedly limited working time, I was more productive because I was more sensual; I lived as a human being must live, passionately interested in everything."

Fay Weldon said that it is more difficult to combine marriage and art, than children and art. She said that with children and writing "the energy comes from the same source ... you're making something out of nothing."

Elizabeth, on the other hand, said that having a baby was "like a love affair," a state in which the energy could "go nowhere else." She could call herself a lover, a mother, even a gardener, but she found it difficult to admit she was a writer. She conveys this in her poem "Trying to Write":

Why am I so frightened?
To say I'm me
And publicly acknowledge
My small mastery? ...
Could I stand up and say
Fuck off! Or, Be my slave!
To be in a very unfeminine
Very unloving state
Is the desperate need
Of anyone trying to write.

This was a challenge she faced to the end of her life.

I AM A WRITER

The last twelve years of Elizabeth's life were spent writing and publishing *A Bonus* (1975), *The Assumption of the Rogues and Rascals* (1977), and *In the Meantime* (1984). She took two extended trips to Canada. The first was for seven months in 1970, during which she turned again to her writing.

Artists discover their voices in different ways. Georgia O'Keeffe discovered the forms she would work on for the rest of her life at the age of thirty when she took a holiday from teaching, locked herself in her room for a few weeks over a Christmas break and laid out big pieces of paper on the floor. She began to crawl around and draw large rounded forms with charcoal. In a letter to her friend Anita, she said that she worked with excitement and some surprise, and when she got the forms down she had to "wonder what it all is anyway ...."

When Martha Graham was about the same age, she too put herself into a period of retreat. She worked alone, encouraged by her friend and musical director Louis Horst, in a bare studio. She moved around the room. She consciously tried to forget all that she had been taught. She rolled and turned her limbs at unusual angles until she began to find the new movements and shapes that became the fundamentals of her dance.

Elizabeth wrote *By Grand Central Station I Sat Down and Wept* when she was pregnant and lived alone in Pender Harbour. She took the raw material of her diaries, the fundamental work she had done in France and Mexico, and found the "concentrated prose" style that she needed to tell her story.

What are the common elements? A period of intense solitude. Work from the body rolled into work from the intellect. A shedding and a stripping away of the known. Deliberate isolation and a self-conscious attempt to work in the unknown. The inward gaze. A descent to a personal truth in solitude.

The inner and outer judging voices are carefully silenced for a time. The new forms emerge. For Elizabeth, thirty years had passed since her first discoveries about prose and now, in 1970, she was attempting to reclaim them in the solitude of a familiar, northern landscape. It was the first time she had been on her own since the birth of her children. She travelled to Gibson's Creek, British Columbia, ten and a half kilometres off the main road from Kamloops and 700 metres up in the mountains. She arrived in February when all was still wintery and white. She writes about trying to hear the rhythm and meaning of her "own voices" again. She describes sharpening herself to the once-familiar smell of pine and cedar woods. She looks again for the wild that she had known as a girl. There is a palpable malaise at her unaccustomed solitude. She makes lists of all the plants she knows, in English and in Latin: salal, kinnikinnick, bearberry *(Arctostaphylos uva-ursi)*, dwarf huckleberry *(Gaylussacia dumosa)*, Douglas fir *(Pseudotsuga menziesii)*, lodgepole pine *(Pinus contorta latifolia)*. She lists the animals she sees on her walks: fox, moose, squirrels. She describes her days as "calm, happy, dread-less." She takes long walks alone in the snow on snowshoes on Campbell Lake. She has little contact with her only neighbours, the Winters family, although she left surprise Easter baskets for the children. Joan Winters said, "We made her welcome but didn't intrude. She told us she was on a kind of retreat. Every day she chopped wood but she didn't know how to pile it, and one day the whole stack collapsed. So we went out to help pile it back up but she wanted to do it herself. She came back one day from around the lake excited at having seen a burl, about a metre across on a tree. She called it a 'witch's bowl.' Once she came to our house in the evening and accepted a glass of wine but she left suddenly before drinking it. We let her be. She told us she wanted to get away."

Elizabeth read a lot, including Thoreau's *Walden Pond*. She returned to her favourite metaphysical poets, Henry Vaughn, George Herbert and John Donne. She read Burton's *Anatomy of Melancholy*.

The rhythms of Elizabeth's adult life had been lived in the tension between her visceral connectedness to others—to her children, to her friends and work colleagues—and her need for solitude in order to write. The purpose of this trip was to "go deep," to experience her inner solitude again. But she had been away for a long time and she worried and wrote, "What if there is no frog at the bottom of the well?"

We witness her struggle to regain her inner spaciousness. A force of character erupts as she thinks about what she wants to write, about how she might rewrite *The Assumption of the Rogues and Rascals* and about daring to write poetry again. But she is not confident, even in her private journals: "BGCS [*By Grand Central Station*]—every possible variation on that theme. Thank goodness that's done. Nothing to say there. The rest is more difficult and of less universal interest. (No, I mean immediate interest. For who's been here before I have? No one. Or do I flatter myself?)"

The journals are suffused with continuing doubt about *how* to write. She rejects conventional plot and character. She struggles on. She describes being bored and frustrated by her notebook: "I've had an aversion to this book for nearly a week—an insurrection. A hate at idea of writing—even just plant notes." She had developed a powerful sense of audience in twenty years of advertising and journalism and she felt that what she now wanted to write about was once again not of "immediate interest." Once again she was going to take on themes that she felt no one wanted to read about. It was time to write what Virginia Woolf called pithily "a new plot." She also articulated the need for witness: "What one needs

(needs? Wants. One can could must do without it) is acknowl-edgement of one's own sacred burden—talent, gift—to help make it real & urgent to oneself." She was working in complete isolation and had to be courageous enough to witness to herself.

＋〜＋

The 1970 journal contains the rough, raw material of some of Elizabeth's final poems. Rhythms push through. Wit and her themes push through. Her pen starts to play with sound, with images and rhythm. She scrawls:

> Scratch scratch
> Clear a patch
> Leave it a minute
> The weeds are in it
>
> ... what then says the hen
> How now my brown cow
> Wit is this
> A cool snow-locked wisdom
> Out of earshot, scream and kiss.
> Calm dead?
> A better compost
> Than most?

Elizabeth, far away from family and friends, was in the landscape of her birth. She wrote: "... how it feels to be me. After wild love, universal love, giving all of love, dishing it out, everybody insatiable for it. O yes, getting it back too ... but ...."

In May, she moved to a cabin in Vermont, not far from her sister Jane. She fasted. She was lonely and self-reflective. Her physical strength renewed as the days passed. She got herself writing again, and returned over and over to her guiding principle of working with the truth "unconcealed": "It's not the skill, the craft that was thwarted but the ability to tell the truth—in the name of kindness? Humility? Humanity? Social expediency? Peace? Pah! ... I had to get through. Children. I didn't."

In mid-July, she experiences a release: "First inkling of a breakthrough. What Bliss. The ferns immediately assume a startling beauty .... The endless opportunities for joy that suddenly take you unawares, releasing you, like a wild bird into uncaged freedom. A bonus!" She continued: "Now I'm at the centre of the world & nothing else matters & everything is all right & a benevolence flows down over everyone & over every petty preoccupation & idiotic anxiety & irrelevant interruption & the painful paralysis is as nothing & how can it ever have been?"

It was a fruitful period of writing, but she could not stay; there were problems with her family in England. She travelled back to London in August, and the next day she took

Rose's two daughters with her to The Dell. Five months later, Rose was again in hospital suffering from an overdose.

Nevertheless, Elizabeth continued to work on *The Assumption of the Rogues and Rascals*. She had previously published two parts of it in the literary journal *Botteghe Oscure*, in 1951 and 1953. When she came back to it again in 1975, she made two significant changes. She made the diction tougher and starker by replacing such phrases as "matted hair" with "lice in her hair" and "ravish" with "fuck." But most breathtaking, she replaced the allusive name "Penelope" with her own name, Elizabeth. Despite frequent lapses of confidence, despite writing of the difficulties of speaking "unmasked straight out of deepest experiences," once again she found her way by putting her "I" at the centre of her fiction. But she faced the old problem of writing without plot and character. Her work was neither essay nor novel. She wrote, "The Book has to have more shape. I.E. beginning, middle and end. Statement, elaboration, elucidation, resolves .... It's too vague just to say here look this is what is like to be me, to be alive now. To have had children, to work, to try to write, to try to love, sometimes to succeed, sometimes not. The conflict between work & goodness, God & the ruthless muse."

The Assumption of the Rogues and Rascals traces the psychological movement of a woman who supports her children, who writes and who is trying to make sense of her experience. It begins in post-war poverty and desolation. The first parts are dominated by world-weary words—*heavy, sad, vomit, cold, boring, gory, sighs, long, slog, fearful.* She uses crucifixion imagery and the language of Christian sacrifice. Then, in a chapter called "Bearing," she breaks free and works at reconciling the end of romantic love with babies and work. We hear echoes of St. Augustine and one of her favourite contemporary writers, Samuel Beckett, in the new simplicity of her language: "To dare to be born. To bear love." We hear the I's self-acknowledgement in "Celebrate! Celebrate! It is not too much to bear a womb." Elizabeth finally manages to write her experience of post-war domestic life in this book. This is the plot summary she liked to perform at public readings: "Once upon a time there was a woman who was just like all women. And she married a man who was just like all men. And they had some children who were just like all children. And it rained all day .... Chapter one: they were born. Chapter two: they were bewildered. Chapter three: they loved. Chapter four: they suffered. Chapter five: they were pacified. Chapter six: they died."

In a Canadian interview she said, "It contains practically everything I wrote since *By Grand Central Station.* I couldn't write much because of what I was doing; occasionally I would get really desperate about that. Well, I was desperate the whole time because I wasn't writing."

In the chapter entitled "The Assumption of the Rogues and Rascals," she describes a woman "with lice in her hair and a faithless lover" who cannot return to a "bed without love" and chooses instead the raw passions of Soho and a philosophy of pain: "All right. I accept. The price of love is pain, since the price of comfort is death and damnation."

Out of this truth, the narrator must create. She calls her pen "a furious weapon," struggles with her need to be loved, with "boredom," a word that recurs often. She also struggles with finding the right prose form and with having the confidence to "keep track of this one female body ...."

As she struggles with her late writing, Elizabeth notes in her journal, "I know nothing. I have nothing to say. But the need to say it nags on."

ARTISTS WITH CHILDREN: ANOTHER LIST

When I asked Carol Shields how she managed to write her early books with five young children at home, she said that she wrote for one hour a day, between eleven and noon. She remarked on the necessity of clearing that little patch in the midst of "domestic order/disorder" so that work can be done. She wrote, "I suppose this is why I love the tidy intricacy of desk drawers, little sections for stamps and paper clips and envelopes and my thesaurus and dictionary handy on their stand. It makes it feel like real work, legitimately taken on." There is a measure of classic Shields' irony here. No need to defend the "real" work of raising children, but tidy paper clips are the necessary defence against doubting the legitimacy of writing. Legitimacy is achieved when one writes the truth.

Loving and nurturing a child is work that requires emotion, intellect, reflection, physicality and empathy. It asks us to listen delicately, to be actively, sensitively, patiently present. It asks us to pay full attention. It is about responding and detaching without being either absorbed or withdrawn. Writing, on the other hand, often requires absorption and withdrawal, though some writers are able to do this in the midst of all sorts of distraction.

I once asked Toni Morrison how she wrote her first novel when she was earning a living as an editor at Random House and raising two young sons alone. She said, "I wrote a list of the things I had to do. I found sixty-three. Then I wrote another list of things I wanted to do. I found two—write and mother my children."

I had a curious chat a few nights ago with a writer whom I had not seen for several years. I congratulated him on the birth, a year before, of his third child. His wife is also a writer. I said, "It's wonderful but it slows one's work down for a while." He shook his head and said, "Oh, it has for my wife; I'm writing pretty much as I always have."

I return to Kaethe Kollwitz, who wrote about the potency of her life with children. Moment to moment there are interruptions and the struggle to find time and concentration. At the same time her sons' faces (literally) fill her work—even her drawings of war and poverty. She wrote in her diary that in the last third of life "... there remains only work. It alone is always stimulating, rejuvenating, exciting and satisfying." Life embraced deepens the work and the reflection. In any event, it is all for such a short time. What is important, I think, is to keep working.

THE MOTHER BOOK

What is still concealed?

Virginia Woolf understood this question. She wrote to her imagination, "... I cannot make use of what you tell me—about women's bodies for instance—their passions—and so on, because the conventions are still very strong."

The Greeks understood this question. Persephone travelled between her mother Demeter on earth and her abductor Hades in the underworld. The Greeks called her the one "whose name may not be spoken."

Elizabeth Smart lived this question. She wrote, "I am afraid to say the important things."

We persist in confronting this question. Hélène Cixous wrote, "The only book that is worth writing is the one we don't have the courage or strength to write."

⁓

The book Elizabeth could never complete was something she called her "mother book." She kept working at it in her diaries. She described childhood scenes. She tried to reconcile herself to the negative mother who could freeze her inside, who could reject her lover, who could reject her book and her creativity. She tried to understand why, even in old age, she called out for her mother in her sleep, why she kept hoping for love.

After a century of psychoanalysis, the subject of the mother is still riddled with taboos. We have few stories about the moments of violence mothers experience in the presence of their children. We have few stories about mothers who admit to wishing they hadn't had children or mothers who desert their families. We have few stories about just-under-the-surface female rage at how mothers shoulder the emotional responsibility for raising children.

Do we know the stories of women who have been denied their children? How widely known is it—after a century!—that

Maria Montessori developed her early childhood education theories and practice while her "illegitimate" son was raised hidden in the country. We have few stories of accomplished women who combine their work with being mothers. We have few stories of self-sufficient and thoughtful and choice-making women who raise confident, independent children.

I can almost, but not quite, understand why the image of a violent or neglectful mother is taboo. But why is the image of a self-affirming, effective mother also taboo? If you doubt this is true, name two great characters in literature who are great mothers and fully realized individuals. I know lots in life. Why are they not drawn as great literary characters? Where are the stories of their inner searches and struggles? Why is the list of Female Characters with a Will Toward Individuality so short? I will not even mention the punishing image of the "super-woman" that has distracted so many of my generation. I once met a writer who had two children, a full-time corporate job, and an apparently successful marriage. She was praised by everyone for her ability to "do it all." But after a workshop with students in which we digressed into a discussion of writing and raising families and making a living, she came up to me and said, "I didn't tell the students that my daughter is in boarding school."

Examining mother relationships and women at work was new when Elizabeth was working. It is still uncomfortable terrain.

Elizabeth chipped away at her ideas in her journals:

The mother is messy, living, terrible, excruciating reality. Known or unknown. The idea. The one having been ONE, welded together. The revenge of the womb. That hopeless never-again-to-be state of well-being. Cast-out cast-out cast-out.

Umbilical. The cord is cut.

Is this brutal rejection ever forgiven?

It's a terrible place, where I want to go. You'd have to repudiate every kind of human love, especially the mother's.

I want to go there ....

What I want to explore is the severance, the necessary severance, of this wonderful completeness—in the womb, perfect, and even for many years after, a passionate connection ....

I'm tangled up in various layers of the mother thought. From pretty and superficial to the deep ugly, murderous.

Elizabeth's 1977 journals work at trying to separate thoughts of her own mother from the archetypal mother:

What is the trembling passionate love for a mother based on? *Not* at all on her merits, character, worth. So why try to describe *her*? Only the desperate attachment that towers over your early life. Often later life too. How can I convey this? It's as vast and inescapable and omnipotent and disastrous as the weather ....

Yet I went on loving her—if this is love. If what a child feels for a mother is love. If it isn't love, what is it? Later, whatever it was was joined to a passionate compassion, a protective pity that tied one in ropes, constricted movement, even thought.

Is it mothers I need to speak about? (If I still cry out at night, aged 63, heard throughout the house, through several walls, still wrestling with infantile anguish, attitudes.) ....

... Hearing, trembling with her cries, her frantic unfair efforts to sabotage me, but going unflinchingly on.

I think I know. I think I understand. Why do I still scream, then?

Here I am in my happy Dell, with the fire going well in the Rayburn. Crocus and Beethoven pleasuring me when I look up, when I listen, a useful rain streaming down in my garden, peace achieved at last: yet after this perfect productive day, I might lie down and the screams recur.

So what is it about? Do I dare to plunge into this journey?

... But life is murder. And art is even worse ....

So dig a grave and let us bury our mother, but not before we've murdered her.

(My poor daughters, my poor daughters, *please* do the same for me.)

Vivian Gornick writes in *The End of the Novel of Love*, "Today even the most ignorant among us knows that murder will not accomplish separation. You can't kill your mother because there is no mother to kill. It's the mother within who's doing all the damage. That's a piece of shared wisdom that the culture knows down to its fingertips."

Elizabeth knows this too:

> I wasn't going to write about *MY* mother—only the passion-
> ate relationship—serving nature?—longer-lingering than
> the most passionate sexual love—and more abused?

She is uncomfortable writing these things. She reminds herself of Margaret Atwood's advice to her daughter in "Solstice Poem": "Be ruthless when necessary; tell the truth when you know it."

And she keeps working at her own difficult truth: "It's easier to abandon your children than your mother—which is the memory of a hope of a perfect human understanding, a oneness of course impossible, but a vivid unforgettable leaping hope, aroused again by passionate sexual love, but that that is easier to get over, being never so perfect as things were in the womb ...."

She worked her rough prose into poetry. First the journal entry:

> The doubts remain, parental doubts, heavy things to carry about. (Did you realize this when you became pregnant, my dear?) ... my mother's desperate fears warning, hold me, keep me inactive, good little girl, perfect little lady.

And then the poem:

> Doubt, parental doubt
> Is a heavy sort of thing
> To carry about
>
> Did you realize this
> When you became pregnant,
> My pretty miss?

But in the end, Elizabeth was unable to find a shape for her "mother book." She doubted its "legitimacy," felt guilty about her own mother, and worried over her technical form. Even after her mother had been dead for eleven years Elizabeth wrote, "Guilt riddles me. How she would suffer if she could read what I have written."

But she found the courage to publish what she did know about mothering—personal and universal—in *In the*

Meantime—just before her death. She did not want to die without speaking honestly about a subject that had been taboo her whole life. In that last collection, she published the fragment *Dig a Grave and Let Us Bury Our Mother*. She also published a poem about being a mother to the daughter she lost:

Rose Died

Unstoppable blossom
Above my rotting daughter
Under the evil healing
Bleeding, bleeding.

There was no way to explain
the Godly law: pain
For your leaping in greeting
my failure, my betrayal,

shame or my cagey ways,
protective carapace;
blame for my greeting leaping
over your nowhere place.

Spring prods, I respond
to ancient notes that birds sing;

but the smug survivor says this is after the suffering,
a heavenly lift, an undeserved reward.

Your irreversible innocence
thought heaven now, and eternal,
was surprised, overwhelmed
by the painful roughly presented bill,

the hateful ways of the ungenerous.
But, loving the unsuspecting flower
could love urge bitchiness
as a safe protective covering?

O forgive, forgive, forgive,
as I know you would,
that my urgent live
message to you failed.

Two sins will jostle forever, and humble me
beneath my masked heart:
it was my job to explain the world;
it was my job to get the words right.

I tried, oh I tried, I did try,
I biked through gales
brought hugs, kisses

but no explanation for your despair, your desperate
Why.

With its smile-protected face
my survival-bent person
is hurtled on by its nasty lucky genes,
its selfish reason,

and greets the unstoppable blossom
above my rotting daughter,
but forever and ever within
is bleeding, bleeding.

By now we know something about Elizabeth. She works with her truth. We see her trying to break the taboos against revealing a mother's imperfections. She does not turn away from pain and guilt and mourning; she knows there is more to write.

She said in an interview, "This is something I've been thinking about. First there is the loving of one person—sexual love—and then the loving of all people. You love your children and then you learn to love other peoples' children. And then there's the trying to do without any of it, without anyone, preparing yourself for death."

Elizabeth wrote about her relationship with Alice Paalen but not about any other relationships with women. In fact, after her love affair with George Barker, she did not write about any of her sexual relationships—with men or women. Her son Christopher has acknowledged her relationship with Sidney Graham in an article published in *Granta,* and Michael Wickham spoke affectionately about his relationship with Elizabeth. Several women with whom she shared relationships in London spoke to me privately but did not wish to be quoted in a book.

Jacqueline Dumas, a writer and owner of Orlando Books in Edmonton, also spoke with warmth about her year-long relationship with Elizabeth when Elizabeth was seventy years old and Jacqueline was thirty-seven. She said, "Lots of women were attracted to her. For me at the time, my relationship with her was everything. I would not have started writing if it weren't for Elizabeth. She treated everyone's writing with such seriousness. She appreciated wit and if you said the right words she was sexually aroused by beautiful language. Everything she did was sexualized but her authentic self was in her writing. When we got too close she would become angry; she was seeing a man too that year. Her notes to me were always unsigned and we had to be discreet. No one could know about us." Jacqueline paused reflectively. "Still, that relationship opened me up wide."

Elizabeth's lovers spoke with tenderness and affection and a kind of head-shaking pleasure at her intensity and her passion, her generosity, her wit and her love of language. Most understood that their relationships with her had to be transient. It is impossible to know why Elizabeth never felt compelled to write about any of her other relationships. Perhaps she simply wished to protect her children's privacy while they were growing up.

She wrote about her body's sensuality to the end of her life. In her last journal, she expressed the desire of her old body for a young lover:

> Old age, aging, growing old, is what I must mention, and the severing of the ties, the divesting oneself of the love of created objects which doesn't necessarily mean that it might not be healthy and hygienic mentally and physically to take a young vigorous lover, would fate bring one to hand. (Ah me, I'm not sure about this, at all, it's pride mostly, fear of humiliation, that stops me from exploring

the possibilities.) It is curious, though, to be ugly, fat, not
seen as a rival by others who are love-objects, even a has-
been, though I never was a been—

It was another bit of the inner ice chipped at but not really
broken.

THE LAST DIARIES

Work while the day lasts because the night of death
cometh when no man can work

Isabel Rawsthorne was a model for Picasso and Derain in Paris
in the twenties. There is a sculpture of her head in the Tate
Gallery. The chin is tipped up, eyes to the sky as if the firma-
ment were her own creation. The sculpture is strong and proud.

She was living in an Elizabethan cottage with a big barn
converted into a studio when I met her. Bars were fixed to
the inside walls of the house to help her walk and she moved
along the edges of rooms like a shadow. We sat in the sunny
front porch looking over a field and she kept disappearing for
a nip of sherry. She told me about Elizabeth's visits to her

garden and about meeting Elizabeth in Soho for drinks. They liked to talk about art and to exchange plants. After a while she handed me a big key and said, "Why don't you go out to the studio and look at my work?"

I walked to the end of the track and swung open the heavy wooden doors on a large, long room filled with sketches and stacked canvasses. Thin spring light buttressed the walls. Dust spun in the low slanted sunbeams. Charcoal drawings were tacked up the length of the walls: study after study of ballet dancers, hands and toes lifted to the sky, pointing to the grave, a room full of woman's bodies in all the attitudes of dance.

When I finally came back, Isabel was standing stiffly in the doorway of her cottage. She said, "Well, if you liked that, you'd better go upstairs and see what I'm working on now. I can't climb the stairs today. You go, look at my work."

At the top of the narrow, worn, dipping staircase was a plain, light-filled room with a bare wood table. A dead thing, a little grey mouse with a long tail, lay arranged on some dry leaves and grasses on the table. There was a half-finished canvas standing to the side and the dead mouse was lightly sketched in, the ghostly beginning of a *nature morte*.

When I came down, she said, "I can't think of anything else to tell you about Elizabeth. She was always so alive."

I had visited so many old women. They lay in their beds, they struggled around their kitchens, along the walls of their homes. They showed me their work. Even if they couldn't show it themselves, they made sure that I saw it. As they talked of the old days their eyes were alight and alive with memories of lovers and art and pubs, so many of their artist lovers dead, long dead.

After that visit with Isabel Rawsthorne, I sat by the gate of the cottage in the sunshine to wait for a taxi to take me to the train. It was late summer, and already cool. I tried to think of all those wonderful sketches of floating ballet dancers, but instead what I saw and still see with burning clarity was her work-in-progress—a charcoal sketch of curling brown leaves and a dead mouse.

For a long time after I met Isabel Rawsthorne I couldn't understand why the visit left such an abiding impression. I think now that it was her insistence that I see her work. Through isolation, illness, the physical limitations of old age, her work was essential. Her work sustained her.

I feel this same energy when I read Elizabeth's late journals. As I read them I hear the familiar voice and the lifelong preoccupation with truth. She creates the character she wants us to know: "If I keep track of this one female body (mind, soul, collection of what nots, same as everybody) and observe faithfully O truly, I'll tell all .... Be stronger, ever so."

There was always an urgent need to write. This is the blessing and necessity of work. To work means to enter the aporia willingly, to be open to the necessary confusion. To work means to remain true to one's essential solitude and truth. Elizabeth kept working and she kept putting brackets around her doubts: "What I want to write about is there .... Women, children, home, and the 97 positions of the Heart, lying low .... I shall just *have* to be brave & go ahead in all my embarrassing obsessions & my heavy, red-nosed self-examination. It would be despicable. Wouldn't it? (Would it? Convince me, in any case I am trying to convince myself) to speak generally of Woman ...."

＋〜＋

In the final years of her life there were many letters from friends and fans of *By Grand Central Station I Sat Down and Wept*. There were thank-you notes from the many people who stayed at The Dell. They wrote of the intense atmosphere Elizabeth created and told her that going back to their usual lives was like going back to "old clothes and porridge." They called her a "courage-teacher" and told her she "restored" them. The young people of Bungay near The Dell felt that she was the centre of all that was interesting in their lives. There are letters from people in various forms of extremity asking for money, for succour, for encouragement. Elizabeth was a great giver, often at the expense of her own time and resources. In the last years there were literary readings and parties and what Elizabeth called "the beginning of nice things happening again." But her closest friends and her children also spoke about how she sometimes lamented not having given more time to her writing. Nevertheless, she worked to the end.

THE END

In the final selection of *In the Meantime: Diary of a Blockage*, Elizabeth describes in spare prose, and in brackets again, psychic and physical changes she experienced as she aged: "(I was an obedient daughter to my body—but I needed it to make good babies, look after them—no that's over, but old habits die hard. *Kill* them.)"

She was interested in her aging, as she was always interested in everything. She observed the "decay creeping from within" and how "you are just a funny old bit of paper flesh that bears no relation to the earlier you." She had things to say about getting old: "The womb had duties, urges, necessities. Old age does too. The *spectacle* of an old woman who isn't kind, sympathetic, unselfish is painful, ugly. But separate this cozy creature from the mad, obsessed artist-monkey within, who takes the balm out of days and never rests, whose frustrations rise to shrill unheard screams as time runs out."

Her final work remains gripped in her lifelong struggle with self-confidence and with a "hatred" of her work. She fought the feeling that "circling somewhere around me out there" was hate, a rejection of her subject matter, a rejection of her style, a rejection of her creativity. I believe that her best work was in *Dig a Grave and Let Us Bury Our Mother* and *By Grand Central Station I Sat Down and Wept*. Both these works were written in periods when she was deeply exploring her body—the first in a lesbian relationship, the second in a heterosexual relationship and pregnancy. Afterwards, in *The Assumption of the Rogues and Rascals* and her poetry, she often wrote of women divided from their own creativity, especially when they were isolated. She struggled with how to shape her new work, and about the separation she felt between her work and her body:

> Confidence regained?
>
> Before, I couldn't say "I want to write."
>
> Now, I feel hate circling somewhere around me out there.
>
> Well, the answer to everything was, is always, ever shall be: Become stronger, be braver.
>
> But the conflict is: the body or the work, the what-is-called meaning-no-judgement, art. What is best for one is often what is worse for the other.

In 1982, a few months after Rose died, Elizabeth returned to Canada for the last time. She went to Edmonton as a writer-in-residence at the University of Alberta and then stayed on in Toronto for a second year, spending time reacquainting herself with the country of her birth. Although she met Alice Van Wart, who edited her final prose collection and her journals, Elizabeth found Canada "stifling" and was generally disillusioned with the "poor caged Canadians." She found nothing in Canada worth staying for, and finally returned to her family, The Dell, and Soho.

She was often lonely in those years and she wrote about that. And she could not understand why others should try to hurt her: "The hardest to fathom were the meannesses, the unprovoked aggressions, the hits for no seeable reason, some cancerous gnawing within ...." In her journals she expresses her customary ambivalence about writing the truth of who she was: "The shameful balking of my waddling body, its greedy seizing of cheap comforts. Betrayal. Shame. A secretness so deep it can't emerge .... Avoiding. A void. Where's courage then? It's still impossible to say I'm me."

She asks, "Am I really old? Am I really going to die soon?"

Faithfully she remains true to her first love—the English language. Poetry is comfort, self-reflection, growth, art. Time fleets away. Words, spoken and written, are her meaning and necessity:

> Now I lay me down to sleep.
> Regret—mostly for the slow too stately way of words spoken. (Written, they go off on their own life, find their right time, like seeds, whirling, floating, snapping, bursting, lying low for generations 'til conditions are right ....

Against the immortality of art, Elizabeth sketches the passage of time and the mutability of her life, like a charcoal drawing of a little grey mouse arranged on dry leaves:

> Fade away, fade away, friends, and when you are faint enough, the ink almost illegible, they come along to disinter you, less than whole, now, hardly resurrectable.

Years before, she had written to her friend Didy: "... this

shedding of every possession, even the human meaning in things, is the kind of pain that leads somewhere—so though maybe I'll never be a female Saint, yet maybe I'll learn how to die (the Good kind of Die), and it's not something I resent, at least in the pact of Fate & Circumstance & God."

Does anyone ever feel one's life work is complete? That one understands? Perhaps some people do. I have sat with dying aunts who wanted to tell me what they knew. I have heard their desire—"if it is meant to be"—to do a little more, to live a little more. I have heard women say, "Life is precious at the end, there is nothing else." There were things Elizabeth still wanted to write. She spent a lifetime trying to speak out and there was more to say. She wrote to the very end. She knew she had heart disease, but she lived as if she were ready for anything. She left her last hospital tests early and told her old friend Hase Asquith, "I have spat. I have pissed. I have shat—what more could I do. I told them I was leaving." She took special time with each of her children.

She made several photographic trips with her son Christopher. They visited the west country and at one stop Elizabeth was enchanted by a nightingale who sang all night long. She had heard the nightingale's song after the very first time she made love with Varda, in France. It was also the bird that her lover, Alice Paalen, sang about in Mexico just before Elizabeth left her. Now she was hearing it again.

Poets call the nightingale Philomel, from the Greek story of

Philomela who was raped and taken to be married by her sister's husband, Tereus. He hid his first wife, Procne, and cut out her tongue so she would not tell. But Procne wove a message into Philomela's wedding dress. When Philomela released Procne, she killed her own child and served him to her betraying husband. The three were turned into birds: Procne into the screaming, circling swallow, Tereus into a hawk, and Philomela into the nightingale whose song mourns the lost love of a child. People hear many things in birdsong—the old myths, their own stories, laments and sweetness before dawn.

Elizabeth also took a trip to Greece with her second son, Sebastian, and she talked to him about her life. She spoke of her lost cabin on 200 acres in Canada. She saw her daughter Georgina and her children, and arranged to be with them for a birthday party.

She went to Soho. A young Canadian woman named Tessa was working at The Coach and Horses, and Elizabeth encouraged her, as she always encouraged the people around her whether they were friends or strangers. Tessa said, "Elizabeth was a heroine. She talked to me a lot. She wanted to know why I'd left Canada and she encouraged me to *live*."

≁

The day I met Geoffrey Bernard at The Coach and Horses, he was standing at the bar telling an amusing story about betting on triplets. He had difficulty talking about Elizabeth. "What's to say?" he said. "She lived. We had a few laughs. She died." I waited and listened to him telling his stories to an admiring circle in the pub. There was something he wanted to say, but perhaps he would not say it. As I started to leave, abruptly he turned away, leaned over and said quietly, "Liz discovered at the very end what she was searching to know her whole life, that she was a poet." It was important for him to say that. All the rest didn't matter.

Elizabeth died alone in The Copyshop on Peter Street. The night before, she had seen old friends in Soho, told stories and recited poetry. This was the language-soaked life that she had created for herself; it was a life of self-exile from Canada, a life with her children, her friends, a life of writing. There were "duties, urges, necessities," not only of the womb but of the word. She wrote in her final journal:

> It's getting desperate. Time gallops. Rivers run dry, etc., etc. Old Age and Death—Old Age and Death.
>   OK. That's OK. the fading away—not pretty, but natural.
>   Only I've left my duties so LATE. A thing not done.

CODA: PAST AND FUTURE

Today young women are artists and raise children. They find ways to get themselves organized with daycare and babysitters. Most important, they call themselves artists. They are proud of being mothers. They know how to decide what they want and they are learning to create the conditions they need to accomplish it. They are learning to create communities for themselves. They are discovering different, more creative, rhythms with which to combine their work and domestic lives.

Recently I was teaching myth to a group of high school students when, in the middle of the discussion, a student asked, "Are you married?" After everyone laughed at her apparent non sequitur, I told her I thought it was an important question. I asked her if she thought she might get married, if she wanted to have children, if she wanted to write. She said, a little embarrassed, "Yes ...." Then the whole group—young men and young women—talked about creativity and raising children and making a living. We talked about the truth of it, as openly as we could.

Doris Lessing reflected in Kate Millet's *Flying*: "The most curious thing is that the very passages that once caused me the most anxiety, the moments when I thought, no, I cannot put this on paper—are now the passages I'm proud of. That comforts me most out of all I've written. Because through letters and readers I discovered these were the moments when I spoke for other people. So paradoxical. Because at the time they seemed so hopelessly private."

The hopelessly private is buried in all of our conversations. The hopelessly private is in our reading and at the heart of *alathea*. I am grateful to that young student for her courage in speaking up.

I am grateful to Elizabeth Smart for her writing, and for her unwavering commitment to the truth of her own experience and what she called "this single female body." She wrote: "I have to trust, to follow the inspiring lead & have faith in inscrutable ways."

ACKNOWLEDGEMENTS

I would like to thank first Elizabeth Smart's children, Georgina Barker, Christopher Barker and Sebastian Barker, the other members of the Smart and Barker families, and the many friends of Elizabeth Smart who spoke with me about Elizabeth and about their relationships, their work, and the historical times.

I would like to thank Lorna Knight and Catherine Hobbs at The National Archives, and my first researcher Sally Kellar.

I would like to thank Carol Shields and Barbara Moon for their generous sharing of wisdom and craft.

A special thank you to Madeleine Echlin, who worked in the archives, travelled with me, selected photos, read several drafts of the manuscript and added her lived insight into women's changing roles in the twentieth century.

I would like to thank Janice Williamson and Rima Berns-McGowan for insightful reading of the manuscript and discussion of the issues.

A special thank you to Sandra Campbell for careful reading of many drafts of the manuscript and ongoing sensitive, courageous discussion.

Thank you to Althea Prince and to the fine team at Women's Press: Rebecca Conolly, Allyson Latta and Susan Thomas.

A grateful acknowledgement of the scholarly work on Elizabeth Smart by Rosemary Sullivan, and Alice Van Wart's sensitive editing of Smart's writing and journals.

To Leslie and Alan Nickell, and Adam and Ann Winterton, my thanks for friendship and intellectual sharing that is generous beyond measure.

And to Ross Upshur, my love and gratitude for discussing and living the issues in this book side by side with me.

LIST OF PHOTOGRAPHS

Page 2: "It's a terrible place, where I want to go. You'd have to repudiate every kind of human love, especially the mother's." *In the Meantime: Diary of a Blockage.*
Elizabeth playing with her daughters at Tilty Mill.
Photo credit: Michael Wickham, author's collection.

Page 68: "A meaningful scream/Between folded womb and grave ..." *The Muse: His & Hers.*
Elizabeth at Tilty Mill.
Photo credit: Michael Wickham, author's collection.

Page 95: "I escaped by a hair's breadth the torpedo ... I waited, with my daughter strapped into my lifebelt ..." *The Assumption of the Rogues and Rascals.*
Elizabeth with Georgina in the Cotswolds.
Photo credit: unknown, author's collection.

Page 101: "I can feel the taste of death in my own mouth."
Diary entry after learning of her father's death.
Elizabeth on a picnic with her family and visitors.
Photo credit: Michael Wickham, author's collection.

Page 135: "I love Rose so much I almost long for a 5th—"
Letter to Didy Asquith after Rose's birth.
Photo credit: unknown, author's collection.

Page 146: "Write, just do anyhow." Diary entry while living
at Tilty Mill.
Elizabeth's children in front of the stone mandala and playing near the abbey after their year in Ireland.
Photo credit: Michael Wickham, author's collection.

Page 149: "Keep small. Keep the perfect drop in mind." *In
the Meantime: Diary of a Blockage.*
Elizabeth looking at dolls at an outdoor shop in Paris.
Photo credit: Michael Wickham, author's collection.

Page 150: "And why should I file office books instead of putting
my child to bed?" *The Assumption of the Rogues and Rascals.*
Elizabeth's children playing beside the deal table she painted
with their names in Ireland.
Photo credit: Michael Wickham, author's collection

Page 196: "It was a rich experience. Don't deny it. Don't denigrate it. Don't say If Only. Suffer." *How to Mend a Broken Heart.* Elizabeth and George Barker on a Saturday night at Bintry House, Norfolk.

Photo credit: John Goddard.

Page 225: "Why shouldn't an old woman fly?" Old Woman, Flying" *In the Meantime: Diary of a Blockage.* Elizabeth at a reading in Canada.

Photo credit: unknown, author's collection

Page 230: "Amazement, wonder, breaks through, stops you in your tracks." *In the Meantime: Diary of a Blockage.* Elizabeth's garden at the Dell.

Photo credit: Anonymous, author's collection.